RED DUSTER RECOLLECTIONS

First published in 2004 by

WOODFIELD PUBLISHING
Bognor Regis, West Sussex, England
www.woodfieldpublishing.com

© Ron Tubb, 2004

ISBN 1-903953-62-6

Red Duster Recollections

A Merchant Seaman's Experiences in World War II

Ron Tubb

Woodfield

The Author, abreast of No. 3 hold, MS *Glengarry*, 1937.

Records indicate that by the end of 1945 some 30,248 British merchant seamen had lost their lives, 4,707 were injured, 5,720 had been taken as Prisoners of War and 530 had been declared missing.

~ ~ ~

These men, or their bereaved dependents, would not be entitled to any compensation, nor would they receive a pension. Merchant seamen were 'civilians' according to the War Ministry.

~ ~ ~

This book is dedicated to my many training school colleagues and shipmates who lost their lives in the service of their country.

The Author as an apprentice seaman, with his mother, Ada.

Contents

The Author and wife, Gwynneth, Porthcawl, 1938.

Introduction

Born in Bridgend, in 1916, Ron Tubb enrolled at Smith's Nautical Training School, Cardiff, when he was twelve years of age, subsequently obtaining an Apprenticeship with the Foster, Hain & Read Shipping Company. His first seagoing assignment was to the SS *Nohata*, carrying cargo to ports in Europe, Canada, Australia and the Argentine.

After sitting his Second Officer examination at the age of twenty, Ron joined the SS *West Wales*, undertaking five voyages. In 1938 he gained his First Officer's Certificate, serving on the SS *Algol*, and subsequently the MS *Glengarry*. His wedding in Bridgend, to his sweetheart Gwynneth, took place during a brief leave, immediately after which he was summoned by urgent telegram to return to the 'Glengarry'— World War II had begun.

In 1940 Ron joined the TSS *Nestor*, a coal-burning passenger liner, carrying evacuee children and their escorts to Australia. Later he was assigned to the *Euryades*, on which, in 1941, he was involved in a hazardous rescue at sea. He gained his Master Mariner's Certificate in 1942, subsequently serving on the *Antenor*, a troop ship bound for the Far East.

Ron then transferred to tankers, serving on the MV *Cymbula*, a key player in keeping Britain supplied with lubricating oils for aircraft, tanks and lorries during this crucial period of the War.

His seagoing career ended suddenly in 1944 when, whilst serving on the MV *Dipladon*, Ron became unwell. This was a bitter blow that he was to meet with courage, fully determined to make a successful future for himself and his wife ashore.

In this informative and entertaining memoir Ron communicates his passion for all aspects of seamanship, giving details of the ships, their ports of call, crews and varied cargoes. He describes the perilous conditions encountered – such as the Liverpool Blitz, the U-boat menace and attacks at sea by enemy aircraft – yet his story is punctuated with highly amusing anecdotes, none of which are likely to have been published before.

1. Beginnings

My mother's family hailed from Lowestoft where her forebears had worked as ship owners and chandlers. Her grandfather was a sailor named Robert Holbrook, from the Revenue Cutter 'Ranger' out of London that sank in a gale off Lowestoft. Robert and a few other crewmen had come ashore in a small boat on 16th October 1822 but, with the coming on of night, a mighty gale came and the 'Ranger' was driven before it. The next morning a wreck was observed on the Haisboro Sands. The event is recorded on a number of gravestones in Yarmouth churchyard. Every one of the remaining crew perished, including the Captain, Robert Sayer.

No harbour existed at Lowestoft then. Later, on the day the harbour was opened, a yacht, the 'Ruby', was the first craft to enter. Her skipper was the same Robert Holbrook and the mate, William Moore: my two great-grandfathers.

Robert Holbrook had stayed on in Lowestoft, working for the local chandler and then, in about 1840, married the chandler's daughter.

One daughter of that marriage married a local trawler owner, by the name of Roberts, who fell on hard times due to ship losses and gambling. This resulted in the family moving to Maidenhead to join a cousin with a boat hire business. Their daughter, Ada May Roberts, was working as a children's nurse in Bourne End when she met my father and fell in love.

My birth in 1916 in Bridgend followed that of my sister, Phyllis Ada, eight years my senior (in Henley-on-Thames) and one brother, George Ernest, five years my senior (born in Cwmbran, a suburb of Newport).

On the day I was born, 28th March, Bridgend lay knee-deep in snow. My father on his return from work had to dig his way into the house, then out again to fetch the midwife, as all the telephone lines were down.

We lived on Quarella Road in a house rented to my father, George William Tubb, for ten shillings a week. Quarella Road joined the end of a 'dram road' where coal in horse-drawn metal drams came on rails from the nearby mine to the town's coal-yard, and thence onto horse-drawn carts for delivery to the townsfolk. When other means of transport were developed the old dram road fell into disuse and became a black cinder path, a favourite for Sunday evening walks.

I remember with pleasure the small plot of land adjoining the house where my father kept his chickens and dog kennels. He was a keen breeder of cocker spaniels and there were often up to sixteen boisterous puppies running around.

My grandparents on my father's side owned The Greyhound Inn at Rotherfield Peppard, where my father was born. The village lay about four miles north of Reading and, as a child, I often spent my holidays there. We took the bus from Reading station, trundling along on its solid tyres behind the driver who was perched in a single cab open to the elements, with a waterproof cloth over his legs. Our destination, the Inn, was a primitive building with an outside earth-closet and a snug off the bar to accommodate ladies. The ceiling above the bar was so lightly insulated that sound of conversation from below often lulled me to sleep.

My father's work with the Great Western Railway had meant his moving to a new area every two or three years, so renting was sensible. This time he had miscalculated, for he remained there as the Chief Clerk on Bridgend railway station until he retired after the Second World War. He could remember when the Station Master always wore a fresh button-hole in his immaculate uniform and every passenger was known to him. When someone arrived late, the Station Master would hold up the train, for customers always had to be considered first.

Bridgend in 1916 was a typical, small Welsh market town in what is now known as Mid-Glamorgan. Originally on the old pack horse route to West Wales, the old bridge is still standing, its shallow steps enabling horses to have a safe grip for their hooves.

Every Tuesday farmers left their carts on the green adjacent to the gasworks so as to attend the cattle market. There were two picture-houses in the town, the Cinema and Palace, both owned by the Isaac family. It was the done thing not only to see the pictures but also to cuddle one's girl in the back row, as there was little other entertainment to be had. A small Woolworths, selling nothing over sixpence, and Liptons the grocers were the busiest shops.

The principal hotel in town was the Dunraven Arms, named after Lord Dunraven, a local landowner whose family originated in Ireland and who had a castle at Southerndown overlooking the Bristol Channel. Years earlier the hotel had been popular with the gentry staying to enjoy salmon fishing on the River Ogmore which runs through Bridgend. In my youth, however, the Ogmore was a dead river, polluted with coal dust from the collieries in the Ogmore and Llynfi valleys. In those days profit was paramount, no matter who or what suffered as a result.

At the age of five I started in the infants' class at Penybont School. On my very first day when we all came out for the morning break I thought that was it, so I ran home. My mother took me back to school before a search for me had begun and I avoided worrying the lovely Miss James, my first crush.

While attending Penybont, I narrowly missed being sent to the dreaded isolation hospital with scarlet fever. Fortunately my mother persuaded the authorities to allow me to stay home, on the strict understanding that I would never go out. There was some relief from my solitude when I slipped away to talk to the milkman's horse or ride with Mr West on his dray. The gentle beast became very attached to me and for some time, once I had returned to school, it would look for me and refuse to move once it reached my house.

Discipline in our school was very strict and, as a result, we could all read and write fluently at a very early age. This may well be due to the fact that teachers were free to chastise anyone who stepped out of line. I am sure that the strict regime benefited us in later years.

Mr Owen, the much liked and respected Headmaster at Penybont, had been an officer in the First World War and had one built-up shoe, due to being badly wounded in the conflict. Another teacher, Mr Aubrey, who tried without success to teach us Welsh among other subjects, was very fond of using his cane. On one occasion he approached me from behind, looked at what I was writing, and gave the back of my head a hard blow. My face hit the desk and my teeth cut my lip. Seeing the damage on my return home, my mother stormed up to the school; had she caught Mr Aubrey that day, he would have regretted it. Yet I was not in trouble as often as my good friend, Granville O'Brien.

When the exams came around for the Eleven Plus somehow I failed, why, I could never understand. Many years later I was told that vacancies were limited and many, in spite of good marks, were failed for lack of places. Granville, however, passed with ease and went on to become a schoolteacher himself in the London area.

Shortly after this disappointment my father received a letter from Cowbridge Grammar School giving details of their entry examination for which I was eligible. In the meantime I had also taken an examination for entry to the Smith's Nautical Training School in Cardiff, for I had decided from an early age that I wanted to go to sea. When the results of both examinations were received I came top for the Grammar School just ahead of my school friend, Douglas Meldrum, and had also passed for the Nautical Training School.

So now I had come to the watershed in my life and what to decide. I thought: "if the sea is in me, I had sooner start now." I was twelve and a-half years of age. Douglas was delighted with my decision, as he could now take my place at the Grammar School.

I enrolled at the Smith's Nautical College in Cardiff in 1928, travelling there every day by train. Luckily, thanks to my father's occupation, the price of my season ticket was greatly reduced.

The school was located in a section of the Cardiff Technical College in the Cardiff Civic Centre. Its instructors were mixed, comprising both civilians and officers. Those for the first two years of the course were civilians, as they were compelled to teach all basic subjects, in addition to marine subjects, to students up to the age of fourteen. I was the youngest in my class.

Marine subjects introduced during the first two years included signalling, ship construction and meteorology. We also went once a week to Llandaff where the college had a small shed and two thirty-two foot naval cutters. There were also two boat davits that enabled us to practice mooring and hoisting and lowering the boats. These subjects stood me in good stead in later years and I shall always be grateful for this.

During the third year we were in apprentices' uniform, with small red tabs on the lapel to indicate we were in training. Also, now, our instructors were all retired Naval Officers. The Headmaster was an ex-Naval Captain J Davis, and the class instructor a retired Lieutenant Commander W Johnstone.

Another essential part of our training was swimming. The first time we went to the baths we were lined up and asked whether we could swim. Luckily my best friend, Bobby Smith, went first and was an expert in the water. When I was asked, however, I answered "No", so was pushed in and then rescued by an instructor. The swimming tuition was ruthless, but it worked.

Within a month we could all manage to swim a length and were subsequently entered for the Bronze Medal exam. Part of the exam required that I stand in the shallow-end, with my back turned while a brick was thrown into the pool. When ordered, I had to swim to the deep-end, surface dive to find the brick, hold it on my chest and swim backstroke to the shallow end. This I succeeded in doing and gained my medal.

When I had completed my third year of training at the Nautical College I received a certificate to this effect, so now my career could commence.

2. Early Apprenticeship

The first thing to do was to obtain an apprenticeship on a seagoing ship, but this was not easy as a depression was hitting all industry, including shipping. I was overjoyed when, on the 22nd October 1931, I managed to obtain an apprenticeship with the Foster, Hain & Read Shipping Company whose head office was in James Street, Cardiff.

Due to my previous training my apprenticeship would be for three and a-half years instead of four. I still have the original Indenture, as signed by my father. It sets out in full, in legalese, what the Company undertook to provide and my own obligations. My wages during the apprenticeship were to be as follows:-

	£	s	d
1st Year	5	0	0
2nd Year	7	10	0
3rd Year	12	10	0
Final 6 months	15	0	0
TOTAL	**40**	**0**	**0**

We had to provide our own clothes whilst the Company would furnish, and I quote: "meat, drink, lodging and, except in Great Britain, medicine and medical assistance". I was also to have "In lieu of washing, One Pound annually". Today these sums seem ridiculous, but in those days one had to accept such conditions in order to get on in life.

When I received my first instructions to attend a ship, I was glad to find that a classmate of mine, James (Jimmie) O'Brien was also reporting to his first ship, so we would be travelling together to Falmouth. On arrival at the Agents we were informed that we had been assigned to ships laid up on the River Fal and would be taken there by launch.

On reaching the river we saw tiers of laid-up ships all the way; such a sad sight. Jimmie had to report to another ship further upstream so, now, at fifteen and a-half years of age, I was completely on my own for the first time, facing the unknown.

My destination was the "Tredinnick" one of a tier of three, the others being the 'Tregonell' and 'Tregarthen'. All the ships were of the same capacity and were coal burners with triple expansion engines. Each was capable of carrying twelve and a-half thousand tons of bulk cargo. Their hulls were black, with white deck housing and bridge, whilst the funnels were black with a large white "H" for Hain.

It appears the Company was started by a consortium of entrepreneurs, the principal ones being Foster and Hain, all of whom came from the St Ives area of Cornwall. Their forebears used to own sailing schooners and ketches, trading between this country, the coast of Europe and the Mediterranean, with cargoes of Welsh slate and China-clay. Once steamships became fashionable the enterprises amalgamated, thus giving them the ability to carry cargo throughout the world.

On my tier of ships there was a Chief Officer, named Jones, a Chief Engineer, a Steward who also served as a cook and four first-year apprentices. In the early 1930's there was a worldwide depression, so ships were laid up in their hundreds in practically every estuary. In the Fal alone I counted twenty-eight ships, whilst in the Dart there were many more. Our ship was moored just above the King Harry ferry opposite the estuary to the Lamorna and overlooked beautiful countryside.

We, as apprentices, were engaged in chipping off rust in the holds with chipping hammers and scrapers by the light of Colza oil lamps. Then the metal had to be painted with red lead paint. By the end of our day's work, 9 a.m. until 5 p.m. with an hour for lunch, we were quite dirty and in need of a bath. This consisted of standing in the bath, with a bucket of lukewarm water. One started from the top....

One day a piece of rust entered my eye, for we were not supplied with goggles. The Mate took me to Truro Hospital where, after eye-drops, the piece of metal was extracted with a magnet. Nowadays employers are bound to take precautions regarding their employees' health – a good thing – for in my early seafaring days the employers had only to disclaim all responsibility in order to be freed from any liability.

A great bonus for us at that time was that we had ample and wholesome food, as our Steward was an excellent cook. The ships had been tied up for years and their hulls were covered in mussels below the waterline. I used to climb down into the dinghy, knock off a few mussels for bait and fish for small whiting which were in shoals. My catch greatly pleased the Steward and also we had lovely fresh fish to eat.

After about three months on the Fal I received orders to go home on leave before being allocated to my first seagoing ship. My mother was so much alarmed by the callused state of my hands, their fingernails full of red-lead paint that I hastened to reassure her of my excellent health. She was a wonderful woman who always found time for others, but the prospect of my imminent departure to travel the world was hard for her, as her nest was bare - all the chicks having flown.

Two weeks later I received orders to report to the Head Office in James Street, Cardiff. There I was informed that I was to join the SS Nohata in Barry the next day, as a junior apprentice.

All the ships owned by the Company started with "Tre..". But the SS Nohata, it appears, had been built in accordance with P&O specifications to be chartered by that company for far-east cargoes. P&O had rejected the ship, as she was not fast enough, but her name had never been altered.

The dock where the 'Nohata' was moored was full of ships loading, surrounded by coal hoists, and everything was covered in coal dust. To my untrained eye, the scene resembled bedlam; each time that a coal truck was tipped, its contents streamed down into the hold and plumes of dust flew everywhere. Even the water was covered and one could easily have inadvertently stepped off the wharf. Reporting aboard, I was taken to the Chief Officer who led me to the apprentices' cabin and advised me to put on my dungarees as soon as possible.

The accommodation for four apprentices consisted of a small dining room with a table, one fixed bench, one portable bench and a cupboard for our rations. Entry to our quarters was via a teak door from the deck passageway with a step of about fourteen inches. This step, I discovered in due course, was essential. Our sleeping quarters led off the dining room and had tiers of two bunks on either side. Underneath were four drawers and a small dressing table with a mirror. Next came the bathroom and a separate toilet, reached by a high step designed to prevent any water entering the sleeping area.

I was delighted to find that the second apprentice to come aboard was Cyril Smith, the elder brother of Bobbie Smith, a classmate of mine in the Nautical School.

We left port once loading was completed and sailed down the Bristol Channel, leaving a trail of coal dust in our wake. As soon as we were under way the ship was thoroughly cleaned and the Mate had us all washing the deck rails with a soda-water mixture, a method of cleaning called 'Sooje Moogie'.

The crew consisted of the Captain, three officers, four engineers, four apprentices, boatswain, four sailors, four ABs and a ships carpenter. On the engineers' side there were nine firemen and a donkeyman. Five catering staff included the steward, cook, cabin boy, mess room boy and galley boy. The cabin boy looked after the officers' and captain's quarters and served at table during mealtimes. The mess room boy did the same for the engineers, whilst the galley boy assisted the cook.

After a couple of days on day work, the Mate sent for me to ask if I had settled in and whether I had any previous experience of ships. He was delighted when I told him I had been fully trained, including navigation. I soon found out why, for the next day I was on 'watch on watch' to replace a sailor who was put on day work.

Watch on watch was four hours on and four hours off, with a change of watch occurring in the two 'dog watches', four to six and six to eight. This enabled the deck crew to be put on day work to maintain the ship's paint, ropes and other gear.

Being on watch on watch meant that one was on duty eighty-four hours a week, a bit of a shock to me as I was used to a good night's sleep. Now I had no more than four hours sleep at any one time, but I soon became used to the routine.

A watch at night consisted of two hours wheel, one-hour standby, and one-hour lookout on the forecastle head. By day we were expected to help the deck crew on the two hours not at the wheel, as no lookout was required during daylight hours.

During our night standby hour we used to study by lamp-light with one eye on the clock, for it was a serious crime to be late on relief. The man on the last hour's standby had to call the next officer on duty and the next three members for the next watch. Today this regime might seem unacceptable, but in 'the Thirties' it was normal and did us no harm. Members of the crew were glad to be employed during an economic depression when many people were out of work. Many of the deck crew actually held Second Mate certificates, but were glad of a job as an AB.

3. Early Experiences at Sea

Another result of the Depression was that a ship's running costs were kept to a minimum, especially those allocated to catering. We were on 'Board of Trade' rations, but these provided perfectly adequate nutrition. They included a one-pound cob of bread per day, one and a-half ounces each of tea and cocoa per week, two ounces of butter, a pot of jam every three weeks and one tin of Nestle's sweetened milk every three weeks. To enable us to put milk in our tea we punched two small holes in the lid of the tin, one to blow into to force sufficient milk out of the other hole. We then sealed the holes with matchsticks to deter cockroaches, of which there were many, from entering the tin.

Ships had only ice boxes in which to keep meat and other perishables. After about eight days storage the meat would have a very dubious appearance so it was converted to 'salt tack' with the remaining vegetables. When that ran out, the meals consisted of salt beef or pork with potatoes, beans or peas, the latter being kept in bags in a very dry state. When our Steward calculated the victualling bill for the voyage, as required by Head Office, it worked out as one shilling and one-half penny per person per day.

Our fresh water was kept in a tank in the 'tween deck [the space between the decks of a ship] and was carefully kept for cooking and drinking purposes only. For bathing one took a bucket down to the engine room and asked the engineer on duty. He filled the bucket from some equipment that steamed to distil seawater. This brew was all right for bathing, but was dead water and horrible to drink.

The SS Nohata was bound for Vancouver via the Panama Canal; I remember rotting tree trunks protruding from the canal's waters, for they had not fully rotted when the valleys were flooded. The ship was controlled through the locks by the use of 'mules'. These were large pieces of machinery running on rails, with winches to control the ropes and keep the ship from scraping the sides of the canal.

When we arrived in Vancouver we tied up alongside a large grain silo to commence loading wheat (hard wheat, for bread making). That first day I received a surprise, for Cyril Smith told me I was wanted on the telephone. I had been tracked down by Mrs Speck, a neighbour in Bridgend who had written to her sister in Vancouver telling her the name and destination of the ship. I was taken for a lovely meal out and learned that her husband worked in the mines in the mountains of British Columbia.

It took about two weeks to load the full cargo of wheat and as we had sailed from England in ballast, due to the recession, no ships cleaning was needed. On the way out we helped the ship's carpenter to construct containers of two-inch deals between the 'tween decks and the upper decks, as well as along the centre line in the holds, in order to minimise the surface area of the grain. These constructions are required as during a voyage grain settles leaving a loose surface that is hazardous. Grain in the box-containers settles and prevents the remaining grain from moving.

Shortly after leaving the Panama Canal on our return voyage, the Second Mate asked if I had been seasick. I told him "No" but that I felt off-colour. As soon as I had left the wheel to help on deck, the Bos'n told me to go under the forecastle head and paint some cargo blocks with red-lead paint. What with the up-and-down motion of the ship's bows and the pungent smell of paint in a confined space, I succumbed at last to seasickness much to everyone's amusement; but I was never sick again.

We then received our orders to go to Alicante in Southern Spain. It appeared that their crop of hard wheat had failed. On arrival in Alicante we found that there was no port equipment to discharge bulk grain, so it was done by hand using sacks that were loaded onto rail trucks to be taken away each evening.

We were in Alicante for three weeks to discharge part of our grain cargo, so the crew had plenty of opportunity to roam the town and enjoy the wines. Some overdid this, becoming more than a little the worse for wear, and had to be brought back aboard by the local constabulary.

Leaving Alicante, we proceeded to Malaga to discharge the remainder of the cargo and found that the method for discharging our grain was the same, so we could all look forward to a further three weeks in port.

Malaga served as the ferry port for North Africa, with the ferry running every other day. The only other ship in port besides ours was a German tourist liner; in those days Malaga was completely unspoiled. I used to climb the hill behind the town up to an old Moorish castle, covered in climbing roses, from which vantage point I could view the town and port beneath me, and the seas that were a wonderful blue.

Horse-drawn landaus, driven by coachmen, with richly dressed families within, plied the streets. If a family included a couple of teenaged daughters, all the eligible bachelors would be eyeing them. We also made eyes at them, much to the amusement of the girls and the annoyance of the parents.

On Sunday evenings it was the custom for the local young ladies to walk in the town gardens, accompanied by their duennas. They walked clockwise around the gardens, while the local lads walked outside them in an anti-clockwise direction. Of course we joined in, winking at the girls, making them giggle, and getting savage looks from the duennas.

Discharge of our cargo completed, we sailed for home, only to be laid up for three months at the Cadoxton end of Barry docks. At the same time the beautiful 'Herogin Cecily' was also laid up at Barry; she was the last full-rigged sailing ship and sadly a little later was wrecked off the South coast of Cornwall.

Due to a lack of orders, some ships were sailing from Barry in ballast and returning loaded, just to keep them on the move pending an economic recovery. We had orders to sail to Australia and, to conserve fuel, to go at seven knots. This passage took fifty-five days, using 'great circle sailing'. We passed only one ship and sighted one island in the South Indian Ocean.

Our destination was Wallaroo in the Spencer Gulf, South Australia. We had been on salt tack and beans for over six weeks and drank a daily glass of unsweetened lime- juice, a custom still maintained to prevent an outbreak of scurvy.

Thinking back on this, it was amazing that despite thirty-five men living within yards of each other for weeks, there was very little friction; everyone just content to be working.

On our arrival in Wallaroo fresh food was immediately sought and brought aboard. Everyone was looking forward to it, but unfortunately we all succumbed to tummy upsets and were competing for the toilet for a couple of days.

On the first evening the sailors went *en masse* to the town and, as usual, overindulged in the local brew 'Pink Biddy'. This concoction has since been banned, but it so inebriated the men that on returning to the ship they all dived into the dock, fully dressed in their best clothes. I had to assist a boatman in dragging them out and leading them to their quarters. The next day they looked much the worse for wear and could not believe how stupid they had been. In future they always returned sober.

Our destination was Liverpool and our cargo was to be Concentrates, a grey dust dug out from local hills containing some ninety percent metals of various kinds. It was so heavy that the dockers had to use particularly small shovels. The cargo's weight was such that about six feet of it in the lower holds and two feet in the 'tween decks put us down to our plimsole marks.

I subsequently found out that, due to its high concentration of weight, no ship was permitted to do more than three voyages with such a cargo, as it would strain the plates etc. This rule was established after the loss of SS Trevessa. She had sunk without trace in the South Indian Ocean and two months' later a lifeboat was observed stranded on the south-western coast of South Africa, containing just three survivors.

Their account of the disaster was that their ship had split and that their Wireless Operator had had no time to send a message – they had watched their shipmates dying one by one. I met one of the survivors years later when we were in dry dock in Cardiff. He was our acting Steward, responsible for preparing our meals. He explained that since the tragedy, when he and his shipmates had been starved, he had suffered severe medical problems and could no longer go to sea.

Another voyage in ballast followed, this time to Port Pirie, Australia, a few miles further up the Spencer Gulf. On the return journey we were running short of coal, so called in at Las Palmas in the Canary Islands for 'bunkering' [to take on fuel for the ship's boilers].

A memorable third voyage was soon undertaken, again in ballast to Australia, but this time to load a cargo of grain at a little-known place called 'Ceduna' in the Great Australian Bight. The little town was situated at the end of a single-track railway, there being just one coach from Adelaide every week.

Ceduna's more substantial buildings were the bank and church, both built of stone. Otherwise there were only a few wooden houses and the jetty which had room for only one ship. Loading was achieved by means of flat rail-cars carrying bags of wheat that arrived once a day. The sacks were winched on board and slit open, allowing the grain to pour into the hold while the empty sacks were returned for use again. On the voyage out we had been busy helping the carpenter to install rig shifting boards and feeders, as before. Now, in port, we were busy painting the hull.

I have always loved fishing and had tried my hand but caught only one small fish called a 'trevalli', so had given up trying. However, when I was on the stern, looking into the very clear water at Ceduna, I could see a shadow on the bottom - a shoal of fish. Rushing for my line, I baited the three hooks with bits of fish and in no time caught a couple of dozen, each weighing about two pounds. There was enough for all hands to have some.

I met the parson, the Reverend Wolfe, and his wife who asked me to tea and told me about his work. I discovered his parish was the size of Wales and that it took him two weeks to visit various Stations, give a service, stay overnight and then leave for the next location which could be over fifty miles away. His car was an 'Essex Super Six', the most popular in Australia for its ruggedness and dependability. I noticed that the cellulose had been stripped off the car leaving only bare, highly polished metal. To show why he had done this he took me for a run. We had to drive as directly as possible between two points using a compass, through scrub and thorn bushes that would have ruined any paintwork; there were no roads. I much enjoyed seeing the clouds of budgerigars we disturbed and the occasional cockatoo.

When loading was completed on the last Saturday, the locals had arranged a dance with a three-piece band. Some people had come from up to fifty miles to attend and, luckily, brought their daughters; so we had a lovely evening.

Once again we were England-bound, calling this time at Durban for bunkering. I did not have a chance to go ashore, as the Third Mate was having severe trouble with his teeth and had to attend the hospital. It appears that he had false teeth and that another tooth was growing, causing intense pain. When he returned to the ship he was still doped from the anaesthetic, for they had to split his gum to remove the new tooth.

Back in England we were told to anchor off Falmouth to await orders, as negotiations were being made on the London Grain Market for the best price. After about a week we were instructed to go to Dunkerque in Northern France and, again, found out that there were no grain suckers, etc to discharge our cargo; so we would have another three weeks in port.

On weekends, having nothing to do and not wanting to spend time in bars, I walked along the beach and found the casino (of World War II fame). I went in to have a coffee and found it almost empty except for a couple of families and some young ladies.

The next time I went I took a couple of my fellow apprentices. At that time the new dance, 'The Palais Glide' was all the rage at home and I knew how to do it. So, observing a pretty girl sitting with her parents and not knowing the proper protocol, I took a chance and invited her to dance. Much to my amazement her parents smiled and nodded, so I began to teach her the new dance. This started something, for my pals soon joined in.

The following weekend we returned and found many more people there. We had a wonderful time dancing with all the girls and the proprietor wouldn't let us pay for any coffees or beers, as it appeared we had brought life into the place.

When, during the Second World War, I learned of the evacuation of Dunkerque and the part played by the casino, I could picture it as it had been in better times.

4. Completing my Apprenticeship

We left Dunkerque and sailed to Cardiff, to enter the Mount Stuart dry dock in order for the lower hull to be repainted with anti-fouling paint and for minor engine room repairs. This gave me a chance to go home for a few days.

I have often wondered about how my mother must have felt then. Here I was, her youngest, returning home having seen the world, whilst she had never left the British Isles during the whole of her life. I used to tell her all about the places and people I had seen and tried to make a word picture for her. I am sure that had she been able to travel she would have loved it, for she had plenty of courage.

My next voyage was with a full cargo of coal for the Argentine. They imported a lot of Welsh steam coal for their railways that had been built with the aid of British expertise. We were bound for the port of Ensenada, serving La Plata, on the River Paraná, downstream from Buenos Aires. The voyage out took about three weeks, during which we helped the carpenter to rig the usual feeder between the lower and upper deck in number-three hold (this being the bunker hold). Now came the hard work....

Dressed only in dungaree trousers, sweatshirt and heavy boots, we first had to shovel the coal in the 'tween deck to the outside edges. Baskets of coal were hoisted from the lower hold and emptied into the 'tween deck, where we again shovelled it to the outer edges. When the outer edges were full the hatches were put on in the 'tween deck together with the canvas covers, leaving just the wood square open to the lower hold. By this time the surrounding 'tween deck area was also filled with coal. This work, once completed, meant that there was enough fuel in the 'tween deck to allow us to reach home, and so save money. Furthermore, once we had reached our destination, number-three hold would be empty ready for our cargo.

It was hot work, in the tropics and under steel decking. Copious amounts of water were drunk and our meals served on number-four hatch, so as not to get our dining cabin dirty. As a special concession we all had a tot of rum at the end of the day which, believe me, was welcome.

All this work was in addition to our watch-keeping, eating, sleeping and studying, but as we were young we took it in our stride and ate anything we could cadge off the cook.

Berthing a ship in any of the ports in the upper river had to be carried out carefully, for there is always strong current flowing. The procedure was for the ship to go ahead of its berth, drop the offside bow anchor and steer the ship gradually towards the quay. In the meantime, the small kedge anchor had been slung over the offside quarter of the stern and suspended by two or three turns of two-inch rope, while a wire cable flaked [ran out] along the deck and turns were taken over a bollard.

When directed from the bridge, the correct procedure was to cut the rope carefully with an axe to enable the anchor to drop to the bottom, taking the wire with it. Then, as directed, the wire was fed out, enabling the ship to edge into position between two other ships already berthed. This was the theory, but unfortunately the Bos'n who undertook the cutting of the rope did not complete the job properly and the anchor did not drop. He went back to give it another cut, but as he did so the rope gave way and he jumped sharply out of danger. He was very lucky, for the wire moving fast through the cleat gave him only a slight knock on his posterior. This was enough, however, to make him sleep on his stomach and to prevent him from sitting down for the next week.

Once we had reached Ensenada and the cargo discharge was complete, the next operation was to clean ship. We anchored in mid-river off Buenos Aires and all available members of the crew put on their oldest dungarees and descended into number-one hold. We brushed the sides of the hull with banister brushes to remove loose coal dust that was then swept up and dumped in the 'tween deck bunker. The next day damp sawdust was thrown up the sides and over the bottom of the hold, swept up and dumped over the side.

All five holds were cleaned in this manner and, as each was completed, an AB and I helped the carpenter to erect shifting boards and the feeder boxes between the 'tween and upper decks.

Once work had finished for the day, the galley boy had prepared halved salt-beef barrels filled with warm water. We used to strip off, leaving our dirty clothes on the hatch for donning next morning. Imagine about twenty men, all stark naked, washing and making all kinds of remarks about each other's anatomy; this I leave to my readers' imagination.

While we were in Ensenada a local football team challenged us to a match, mainly so that they could put in some practice at our expense. It did not quite work out in the way they had anticipated. Among our crew were a number of Welsh Schoolboy finalists and, together with two apprentices, we mustered a full team. We quickly scored two goals, to our opponents' amazement, so they changed tactics.

I was on the right wing and, at only seventeen years of age and weighing just ten stone, was a target. Two of the Ensenada team attacked me, one from each side, and knocked all the wind out of me. Of course it was not long before two of their team were also limping. When the game finished, I remember that I walked off without a word and declined another match.

Another vivid Argentine memory is of the large meat factories, some British and some American, where hundreds of cattle from the interior of the country were discharged from riverboats. Cows walked in at one end and emerged as sides of beef, or tinned. This was production on a large scale; some five thousand cattle were processed each week.

We had been given three days to clean ship, culminating in washing the decks and cleaning the paintwork. Twice we loaded in Rosario, about two-hundred miles up the Paraná River. There I met an English family and their two most attractive daughters who taught me to dance the tango in a local park. I had never danced the tango before, but with their help was soon able to join in.

The loading of our cargo of wheat in Rosario was done in much the same manner as in Australia. Bags were slung aboard and cut open, allowing the wheat to flow into the hold. The stevedores used razor sharp knives and were adept at ensuring that sacks were not damaged and would be reusable.

On one occasion, due to some local dispute, the stevedores took up sides, shouting at one another. Suddenly one stuck his knife into his opponent's stomach, causing pandemonium. All the others ran off while the wounded man writhed in agony on the deck. Very soon the police appeared, chasing all and sundry, so no more work was done that day.

As the holds filled, men were down each hold shovelling the grain into the outer edges, so that when this part of the loading was complete there would be a fairly level top on the grain surface. They never wore masks and dust was every-where, so I expect many might have suffered with lung problems in later life. The ship could not be fully loaded there, due to the depth of the river, so loading was completed at Buenos Aires.

Leaving the Rosario berth was awkward, so there had to be careful co-ordination between heaving the bow and kedge anchors, in order to ensure that the bow was slightly further off, to allow the current to move her to the midstream. The spring ropes running from each end towards the centre of the ship were held so that she would not move astern into another ship close under our stern. At a given point these springs were cast off and we swung clear.

Loading completed, the grain was again levelled off. The feeder boxes were now completely full, so that any movement of grain during the voyage would be minimal.

Altogether I made three trips to the Paraná and, on one oc-casion a swarm of locusts descended on both sides of the river. The river's banks were covered in them and our decks were a moving mass. They even entered the galley where the cook did his best to keep them out of his pots of cooking food. The pilot stated that this phenomenon occurred frequently.

On my third trip trade was bad and we had to anchor a hundred miles upriver off Villa Constitución to await orders for nearly two months. On this trip, the only memorable occurrence was a '*pampero*', a wind that blows from the Andes across the pampas to the Atlantic. All hands took down our awnings that had been erected to keep the hot sun off our decks and cabins. The *pampero* was accompanied by a violent storm and the skies above us were pitch-black. The storm hit us suddenly and torrential rain battered the riverbanks. No-one could make himself heard above its violent onslaught and, at its height, the ship made a complete turn around her anchor against a strong river current. The next day many pieces of debris floated downstream, including sheds and dead chickens.

Eventually we received orders to proceed to Rosario to load wheat as in previous voyages. Our cargo would be discharged in Liverpool by means of powerful pipe suckers attached to the Rank mill. This was completed in a couple of days and we returned to Barry for another cargo of steam coal bound for Bahía Blanca, Argentina, located a little further south of Buenos Aires and the principal town for a very large area.

My father had suggested that I look up an old friend of his, a Mr Colman, who used to work on the Great Western Railway at Tondu, six miles from Bridgend. I inquired ashore at the Mission to Seamen in Bahía Blanca, run by an English couple. Much to my surprise, the husband told me that the man I was seeking was his boss and that he would tell him of my arrival. I soon received a message saying that on the following Saturday a car would pick me up. The car duly arrived, driven by a chauffeur, and I was conveyed to the Railway Office in town to meet Mr Colman.

I was made most welcome at the Railway Office, but my arrival coincided with a report of an accident that had caused one fatality. It was a revelation to me to watch them discussing the matter in fluent Spanish. Shortly afterwards I was taken to the Colmans' home, a lovely detached residence with a walled garden, and introduced to his wife who was Argentine by birth and their two daughters, one in her twenties and the other in her late teens.

The meal we had was totally different from our ship fare and there were four types of glasses and cutlery at every place setting; luckily I knew the correct procedure. We all conversed happily, as Mr Colman acted as interpreter. He then took me into the garden to show me his beautiful beds of roses stating, to my amazement, that these were growing in British soil. He explained that every time he ordered a cargo of coal he had an agreement with the shipper to include one hundred tons of best English topsoil.

We also looked at photographs showing the railway that was currently under construction towards the Cordillera Delo mountains between Argentina and Chile. Mr Colman had been involved in the project for years and there had been many obstacles to overcome since its inception. To me, one particular photograph stood out from his collection. It was taken from the rear of a train pulling a single carriage, travelling at full speed to outrun a huge wall of water descending from the mountains.

After cleaning the ship and erecting shifting boards again, we left Bahía Blanca and returned to the Paraná River to load, as before.

During this voyage I completed my three and a-half years apprenticeship, on 22nd October 1934, and was put on AB's pay. When I arrived back in Barry on 13th May 1935 I had more money in my pocket for the first time. For those six months my pay was more than twice that of my three and a-half years as an apprentice.

As I was only nineteen years of age, I could not sit my Second Officer examination until I was twenty, so I bought a bicycle – a B.S.A. Sports Tourist with 'North Road' raised handlebars – and set off on a country tour. I met many other cyclists on my way: a man who was chauffeur to a Lord, enjoying something he could never do while working in London and two American girls who were going to take their bicycles home with them, as these were much lighter than American ones.

I then returned to training school for three months intensive revision and finally sat the examination under Captain Burgess, the examiner. The first part of the examination consisted of five days' paperwork on navigation, signalling, ship construction, etc, and all sundry matters relating to seamanship.

The following week there was an oral session at which one was seated on one side of a table with writing pad and paper, whilst the examiner sat opposite with a pile of reference books, a sextant and barometer. He fired questions at the examinee, opening books at random.

At one point, he asked me about loading different kinds of grain into a single hold and how it should be separated. He was dissatisfied with my answer and tried to persuade me to respond in accordance with the book he was using as reference. I explained that I couldn't agree, as his book was an old edition. It referred to wooden bulkheads between a ship's holds to which sheets of burlap could be fixed with nails, separating layers of one type of grain from another. I had answered that in modern ships a small amount of mixing could not be avoided. I discovered later that he called on the office of the Shipping Company where he found out that I was right—burlap could not be nailed at the edges to steel bulkheads. Two weeks later I returned to Cardiff and, much to my delight, I was given my certificate and Captain Burgess stated that my persistence had clinched it.

5. Early Years as an Officer

After a week's rest, now came the difficult part: obtaining a berth. It would have to be that of Third Officer for, although I had a Second Officer's certificate, things were still very bad with shipping and nothing was picking up. I went to Cardiff every day, calling at all the various shipping companies' offices, but there were no vacancies. Even my old Company could not help.

Eventually, thanks to the intervention of my uncle who was caretaker at Merthyr House in James Street, Cardiff, I was invited to meet a Mr Appleton who had an office in the building. It transpired that he was a Marine Surveyor who managed three ships for two sisters living in Penarth who used the income to support a children's home. Thus I managed to become the Third Officer on the SS West Wales and signed on, on 22nd May 1936.

We had a coal cargo for the Argentine again, to be discharged at Bahía Blanca. This time there was a slight variation. We had to deliver two-hundred tons to a small place called Puerto Deseado, on the Deseado River much further south, whose existence was not widely known until the Falklands Invasion in 1988.

The seas were full of large shoals of fish and, as we moved through the water, it seemed as though the ship was passing through a vast, milky-coloured patch as the fish fled away.

As we approached the port, the pilot came aboard. His first action was to issue cards to all the crew, advertising a hotel. We came alongside the jetty, long enough to accommodate two ships and overlooked by two large sheds. The rest of the town comprised a bank, the one and only hotel and some twenty wooden houses. There were seals and shoals of small squid in the river where local people were catching squid in small, circular nets. That evening we found out that the pilot owned the hotel.

The pilot cum hotel-owner was of German extraction. He made only a meagre living, for his only reliable income would be during the annual *fiesta*. Then, a sudden influx of people, some of whom travelled great distances, would fill the town. Large numbers would be obliged to sleep out in the open because of the lack of accommodation.

The coal was unloaded onto the dock by the bucketful, to be taken to the local railway depot for the locomotives. The railway-line ran from Puerto Deseado to a location just inside the Chilean border. Historically, when relations between the two countries had been particularly tense, it had been built to transport troops onto a broad front. Eventually those early differences had been resolved, so the railway and rolling stock had been sold to the sheep ranchers.

I learned that the ranchers, almost all of whom were direct descendants of Welsh settlers, would drive their flocks to Puerto Deseado for shipment to meat processing plants, this activity being timed to coincide with the *fiesta*. The *vaqueros* (stockmen) would spend months at a time out on the *pampa* with their flocks, as each ranch covered a vast area. Individual sheep stations were able to maintain contact with each other by means of short-wave radio.

Leaving Deseado, we returned to the Paraná, going up-river again to Rosario to load grain in bulk, and on to Buenos Aires to finish off loading. This was a procedure with which I was now very familiar, but suddenly something shocking was to occur.

Whilst we were leaving the mouth of the river, we were overtaken by a much faster ship, the 'Duquessa' a Houlder ship, carrying frozen meat bound for Britain. Veering sharply towards us, she collided with our port quarter, causing a gash down on the waterline. She freed herself and proceeded to Montevideo, where we joined her soon afterwards. When we arrived in port we observed that engineers were using burners on her bow, in an effort to free her port anchor that had been forced into the plating.

Our own damage was examined by the local Lloyds Agent and, as we could not proceed with this large gaping hole, he gave instructions to the local shipping people to obtain various materials that were brought alongside in a barge. A wooden structure was erected on the inside of both the hold and the 'tween deck, and a hole was cut in our main deck. Rubble and concrete were then poured into this box until it was full, thus forming a plug that would allow us to sail home, albeit with a four-degree list to port.

We arrived home safely and went into the dry dock in Cardiff for repairs. These took some time, for all the concrete and rubble had to be removed using pneumatic hammers and drills.

As I had been on the bridge at the time, my evidence to the Enquiry into the accident was crucial. Our representative briefed me beforehand and it now turned out that, even though both ships had had pilots aboard, the Masters were still responsible. The Enquiry learned that the 'Duquessa' had hit a sandbank that had recently formed in the channel and had sheered off it, hitting us. The 'Notices to Mariners' state, however, that an overtaking ship must keep clear of the ship being overtaken, so liability was agreed within the day.

I undertook five trips as Third Officer on the SS West Wales. Those were happy days and I signed off on 14th March 1938 in Newport, to sit for my First Officer's certificate. After three months intensive studying I obtained this and at the end of June looked forward to a few days relaxation, for whilst studying at home I had met a young lady, Gwynneth Pothecary, who to me was most beautiful.

One evening, while walking home from the pictures, I was suddenly taken ill and my condition deteriorated rapidly overnight. The doctor came and persisted in pressing my appendix, but I told him the pain was high up on my left side. My mother, who had studied nursing, telephoned a friend who worked as the matron of a hospital. She referred her to Doctor Hodgkinson of Porthcawl who had studied tropical medicine. My own doctor reluctantly agreed to a second opinion.

When Doctor Hodgkinson called, his first question to me was, "What was your last illness?"

I told him that it had been dysentery in Argentina.

"And what treatment did you receive?" he asked.

"Pills, like ball bearings," I replied.

Luckily, I still had a couple of these left in my trunk that he identified, telling my mother that I had colitis. Apparently the dysentery had not been completely eliminated, hence the inflammation of my intestines. He prescribed Glucose D, plus hot and cold compresses. My mother and Gwynneth took it in turns to apply these and in a few hours the pain began to subside and I slept. I was so weak that it took me a further week to get back on my feet.

I was in Cardiff one day, calling on the Merchant Officers' Union office to pay my dues, when I was introduced to a Captain Stewart who asked me if I could help him. He was Captain of the SS Algol, a 'six-month articled ship' [the term applies to a ship excluded from deep waters] that was ready to sail the next day. Unfortunately his Second Officer had crashed his motorbike and his ship could not sail without her full complement of thirteen crewmen. I said I would return home to pick up my clothes and sextant, but he stated "You will not need your sextant, for we are never out of sight of land."

That evening when I returned to Cardiff and went to the dock I could not see any ship, but looking down, there she was. I was met by the night watchman and shown my cabin which was small, but very comfortable. After a good night's sleep we sailed the following morning.

The SS Algol was nothing like my previous vessels, for she was quite small, carrying only one thousand tons of Welsh coal, with a freeboard of about three feet so one could almost touch the water from the deck. Her crew was made up of the Captain, two officers, four deck hands, two engineers and four firemen, all of whom came from the Orkney Islands.

Food on board was excellent, but I couldn't face raw, salted herring for breakfast, so they kindly cooked bacon for me. The crew were all extremely kind, but I found that one was left alone on bridge duty and it was during my watch that we rounded Lands End. I was very relieved when daylight came and we were right on our course.

As she had only about fourteen-foot of draught, the SS Algol could go up the inshore channels of the East Coast and one was able to see the people on the beaches. I must say that the experience stood me in very good stead, as one navigated around fishing boats, not keeping well off as in larger ships.

We were chartered to deliver the coal to the Rosyth Naval Station. When we arrived, Captain Stewart told me I could go off and enjoy myself for a week if I wanted, so I caught a train to Edinburgh. There I met an old friend, Robert Craig Drummond. He had been injured in the 1914-18 War and had practiced dentistry in Bridgend for years, lodging with Henry Starling's mother in Sunnyside Road, with his surgery in her front room. He had since returned to Scotland where he lived with his two maiden sisters.

Mr Drummond was delighted to see me and we had some wonderful sessions around the bars, being met on arrival home in our somewhat inebriated state by two rather irate but considerate ladies.

I rejoined the SS Algol and we left Rosyth for Goole where, sadly, she was likely to be broken up. I returned home after signing off on 29th July 1938.

6. A Better Class of Ship

At this point in my life I felt convinced that a fresh chapter was beginning and that now was the time to look for a better class of ship. I began to peruse the Lloyds Shipping lists and write off to various prestigious companies. After about four months of frustration, a letter to Alfred Holt & Company of Liverpool brought results.

I travelled to the Company's head office in India Buildings, Liverpool, and after a lengthy interview was informed that I would be accepted and would shortly receive my orders. When these arrived they stated that I was to join the MS Glengarry, a ship formerly owned by a small company that had been taken over by Holts.

When I arrived at the Victoria Dock in London I was pleased to see my new ship. She was painted black with white upper-works, whilst her funnel was red with a wide black band at the top. These ships were constructed in excess of Lloyds' specifications and had lifting gear of up to one hundred tons. Instead of being designed for bulk cargoes, they were equipped with two 'tween decks, cool and cold chambers, and a locked chamber for carrying spirits.

Our cargo consisted of thousands of items, from large packing cases down to parcels only about six inches square. In the sheds dozens of stevedores were busy and tally clerks were noting all marks on each item, where it was to be stored and its destination. This system had been perfected over the years and each item had to be loaded so that it was readily accessible when it reached its destination.

I discovered that the 'Glengarry' could carry up to twelve passengers without having to obtain a Passenger Certificate, for which there were strict rules regarding accommodation and life-saving equipment. Her crew was also larger than my previous ships. Besides the Captain, there were four officers, four engineers, deck hands and firemen, as this was a motor ship with a four-cylinder diesel engine. She was not an extremely fast ship, about twelve knots, but was so well built and clean it was a joy to be on the bridge observing the decks, particularly once we reached the warmer climates. This was a completely new world for me and I was eager to adjust to it.

Four days after I had boarded, we sailed for the Far East under Captain Waite, a quiet person who spent many hours on his hobby, decorating items with paint and finishing them with a marbling effect. We would be calling at Suez, Aden, Colombo, Hong Kong, Shanghai and Japan.

At Suez many 'gilly-gilly' men came on board, to sell cheap beads and trinkets. Some were very good at sleight of hand that involved a live baby chicken. Once the pilot and two, compulsory, boatmen complete with small boat were hoisted aboard, we proceeded through the Canal.

At one point we had to tie up to the left bank to allow a convoy of ships going the other way to pass. For this operation the small boat was lowered and the boatmen secured ropes to bollards fore and aft. Now we had to secure the two specially made springs, one heading forward and one aft. These consisted of a length of double constructed, twisted rope attached to a wire hawser. When secured, the rope sections were along the deck and the wires through the hawse-pipe to bollards ashore. As the convoy passed, water suction moved us first forward, then astern, and the rope springs could be seen to stretch, reducing in thickness until each ship had passed, when they eased and the rope returned to normal.

Later, after sunset, special arc lights that had been fitted to the bow were operated, in order to light up the canal ahead. Once we arrived at the Red Sea, the pilot and boatmen left with their lamps and we proceeded on our voyage.

Our six passengers were enjoying themselves, for they dined in the Saloon and had deckchairs on the deck outside our cabins. Unfortunately they stayed up very late and the sound of their voices kept me awake. We had to have the ports open for ventilation, but a quiet word with them did the trick. Many things that happened outside my port entertained me, including encounters between certain planters' wives, taking advantage of their freedom whilst returning to Singapore, and romantically inclined Air Force personnel.

We proceeded towards Hong Kong after some oil bunkering off Singapore. On the way we were warned of a typhoon crossing the Philippines across the China Sea and expected to pass over or near to Hong Kong itself. We monitored the progress of the typhoon using weather reports, our own observations of the wind direction and barometer readings, reducing our speed to avoid the most extreme weather. Even so we were plunging in heavy seas, the front of the ship first completely buried, then rising with tons of seawater pouring over each side. Luckily, before the weather had really deteriorated, we had removed all the forward hold ventilators and sealed them with wooden stoppers and canvas, secured by strong cords.

When we eventually entered Hong Kong Harbour we observed a large, two-funnelled liner up on the rocks, perched sufficiently high that one could have walked under her. We found out that she had been trying to leave harbour and obtain sea room, but had left it too late and been caught. She was Japanese and we were told later that a salvage crew from Japan would be coming out to see what they could do to recover her. Eventually, on our next voyage, we found out that they had used pneumatic hammers to make a skid for the ship, using tons of grease and then, with hydraulic rams, made her slip back into the water. What was surprising was that they had found that she was completely undamaged.

Our wharf for discharging cargo was on the Kowloon side near the Peninsular Hotel. We took a ferry to visit Hong Kong Island and found it to be an amazing place, so many people and all working hard. We then proceeded to Shanghai where further cargo was discharged into lighters, as we were tied up to two 'dolphins' [large, wooden piled constructions for mooring] in the middle of the river. We all had to keep twenty-four hour continuous watch to stop stealing which was a major industry in those days.

Everything was so still and not a sound to be heard until at about 11 p.m. when I heard the Captain shouting, "Get out! Get out!" and saw a Chinese girl hurriedly leaving his cabin. I hadn't heard a sound or seen anyone, so when the watch was alerted we found further young ladies in the crew's quarters, busy earning a living. It appeared that a sampan, complete with *Madame* and a few ladies, had drifted in on the tide, tied up to the stern dolphin that was out of sight of the bridge, and that she and her girls had climbed the ropes without being observed. When they were rounded up (much to the annoyance of our Chinese crew) they went down the ropes so expertly it was obvious that they had done this many times.

In Shanghai we had three new passengers, two Catholic priests and a middle-aged lady who was attached to a Catholic mission. They told me a lot of their work was with baby girls who were not wanted by their parents, for they would be a liability on the family. It appears that the dowry system was the norm throughout the Far East at that time and, if parents were too poor to provide a dowry for a daughter on her marriage, they would 'lose face' in the community.

We then sailed for Mooji, a port in Japan, to complete our discharging. This cargo was hundreds of tons of steel drop plates from old gas stoves and none of us could fathom out what they were for. The Japanese explained that they were for road foundations, but subsequent events proved they were most likely for use as war materials, being of high quality steel. This was 1938 and the Japanese were beginning to sense their superiority over adjacent nations.

While in Mooji the Port Doctor came aboard, resplendent in his uniform, accompanied by two assistants. He ordered all the crew to line up for inspections and then ordered all the officers to take off their caps and bow to him. We refused. Luckily, the Captain intervened and told us to go to our cabins, take off our hats and return. It was only then that we became aware of the fact that, as our badges depicted the Tudor Crown, the Japanese meant us to lower our badges to them in order to show their superiority. When we returned without our uniform hats, the Port Doctor was furious and could hardly contain himself, particularly when some of the crew laughed.

He left, but an hour later returned, stating that typhoid had broken out in China and that all members of the crew would have to provide a sample; everyone was given a small box for this purpose. It is well known that one of the results of life at sea is constipation and many members of the crew were in difficulty. Fortunately, one individual was suffering with diarrhoea and was generous enough to fill all the boxes himself. We had many a laugh over the incident both then and subsequently.

While we were clearing up the dunnage [wood etc used in the storage of the thousands of packing cases and parcels that made up part of our cargo] we found a small parcel that had inadvertently been missed. It was arranged that the package would be flown to Hong Kong, its original destination. I include this minor incident here in order to illustrate how much care was taken of these items, however small.

Leaving Japan we called at Jentai, where the fore and aft peak tanks were filled with soya bean oil, then back to Shanghai to commence loading. We were to have a varied cargo, destined for various ports, with some items in the 'tween decks. Loading was an art perfected over years of experience.

Our next port of call was Manila where hemp was loaded that, due to its light weight, was stacked at the end of the holds, but on our return to Hong Kong we faced a particular challenge. We were loading 'Cassia bark', a highly aromatic product that had to be kept well away from anything that might absorb the smell and also a drum of precious Jasmine oil that required particular care as it was of great value. We loaded this drum in the centre castle, tying it securely so that it could not move.

From Hong Kong we sailed to Saigon, known now as Ho Chi Min City, to load rice in sacks. It is not commonly known that a cargo of rice will generate heat and that it is highly combustible, so instructions for this type of cargo are that it must be ventilated, both vertically and horizontally every six tiers, with the vertical ones reaching the corners of the hatch-way. These ventilators were constructed from bamboo, bound with cross members. In addition, if any sack appeared stained, it had to be ejected, as this could also cause heating. During loading great care was taken to ensure compliance with these regulations. On the voyage home the hatch of the hold con-taining the rice was opened whenever possible. The heat rising up through the ventilation had to be felt to be believed; one could hardly hold one's hand over it.

Leaving Saigon, it was back to Singapore to load raw rub-ber. This was in large bales covered in sacking. The stevedores were having great fun bouncing the bales until one of them was knocked flat and great arguments ensued.

The 'Glengarry' was now becoming quite full, but a special 'tween deck was set apart for the next part cargo due to be loaded in order to keep it well away from anything that might contaminate it. This sensitive commodity was tea that would be loaded in Colombo, our next port of call. All the tea was in parcels, packed in chests bearing special plantation markings, and up to one hundred cases were loaded. Due to the fact that the port of destination for individual cases of tea could be London, Rotterdam or Hamburg, these had to be stowed in tiers, all ending on the hatchway, so that they could be taken out at any one of the three ports.

Another part cargo we loaded was five-hundred tons of Locust Beans, from which oil would be extracted and the residue used in cattle feed. As children we used buy these beans for a halfpenny each and chewed them for hours, as they were quite tough but very sweet.

It was customary for each officer to be given a small parcel of tea in recognition of the great care that was taken with the tea plantations' products. My gift contained Broken Orange Pekoe, a pure tea, not blended like most teas sold in shops. When I finally arrived home, over a year later, I found that my family did not like it at first, but after a couple of weeks they grew to love it, for it was a beautiful golden colour and unlike anything one sees these days.

7. And So to War…

As I had been away a year, I contacted Naval Control to ask them if I could go home (MS Glengarry was a listed ship, so she came under direct Naval Control). They telephoned me and stated that I could go on "twelve hours' notice". This meant that when I received my orders I would have to leave home within twelve hours and proceed to wherever I was ordered. I agreed, leaving by train from Paddington and reaching Bridgend on the Tuesday morning. Merchant Navy Officers never wore their uniform ashore, but now it was compulsory. When I appeared home my parents were surprised to see me as an officer.

After seeing my parents, I visited Gwynneth who lived six doors away. I asked her what she wanted to do: whether, in the circumstances (i.e. the difficult times ahead) she preferred be single or married. I was overjoyed when she said she would marry me. How extraordinary it was that, after travelling the world and meeting many young ladies, I had found my ideal partner only fifty yards away!

The next day I went to the Registry Office (a church wedding could not be considered due to the time required for reading the banns). I informed the Registrar of my twelve-hour notice order and he kindly agreed to schedule the ceremony for Friday. He had a laugh when I was unable to give him Gwynneth's middle name, but it was something I had neither known nor even inquired about. I had to rush home and return to tell him it was 'Lilian'.

When the great day arrived, Friday 8th September, I put on my uniform and walked to town with my mother and father. Gwynneth's mother and father were also there, although her father was a very sick man, due to his time in the trenches in France during the 1914-18 War.

After the ceremony, the first recorded with the groom in uniform, we faced the problem of the honeymoon. I could not go away due to the notice, so we decided to stay with my parents that night. We had breakfast there and then went to my in-laws' house for lunch. We were sitting in their lounge, talking, when a telegraph boy arrived bearing a telegram ordering me to report at once to Southampton to rejoin my ship. An hour later a policeman called, asking whether I had received the telegram and what time I would be leaving. I told him that I would catch the ten o'clock mail that night.

We went to the railway station that was now in complete darkness. When the train arrived this also had no lights. Finding a seat was difficult and I remember feeling my way along the carriage saying, "Sorry, sir" and "Sorry, miss" until at last I found a space. As you can imagine I wasn't exactly full of beans after one night's honeymoon and asked the other passengers in the compartment if they would wake me when we arrived at Bristol. I must have dozed off, for suddenly I was being shaken and someone was shouting, "Bristol Temple Meads". The station was again in complete darkness and it was 12.30 a.m. All the waiting rooms were packed with soldiers, and no-one really knew what was happening.

After about an hour a porter came, shouting: "Train for Southampton is ready". About twenty of us staggered over, found seats and promptly fell asleep. We were awakened by a porter, shouting "Weymouth, Weymouth, all change" and wondered what had happened, for surely we should have been in Southampton. It turned out that there had been two short trains on the same platform in Bristol and we had boarded the wrong one. We explained to the Station Master that we were all urgently needed on our ships and, good for him, he arranged for us to have breakfast at a nearby restaurant and said he'd let us know when to return. An hour later a porter called us, stating that all was ready, and we found that there was a small side tank engine, plus one carriage, at the platform. We boarded and proceeded non-stop to Southampton where taxis were waiting to take us to the long jetty used by all the large liners.

What amazed us collectively was that all the ships were now a light grey from top to bottom, a complete transformation. We learned that one hundred painters had been allocated to each ship, each with a brush and a pot of grey paint, and told to start from the top and work right down to the waterline. As you can imagine, everything was wet and we trod gingerly so as not to touch anything. As we proceeded along the jetty, each man trying to locate his now colourless ship, I was lucky to notice a slightly dented plate – I had found my 'Glengarry'.

Another chapter in my life was beginning, with my country at war, something I had never thought would happen after the horrors of World War One.

We soon left our berth in Southampton and, in the company of two other ships, set sail with a destroyer escort bound for Brest in Western Brittany. It was planned that we travel mainly in darkness, to arrive off the port at daybreak. This was our first experience of travelling in complete darkness and keeping station was difficult, for our sailing instructions were merely to keep close and follow the warship.

We arrived safely and went alongside to discharge our cargo of Crossley Workshops, each weighing eight and a-half tons, bren-gun carriers and twenty-five horsepower Morris Commercials with a limber and twenty-five pounder guns behind. We also carried a number of armoured cars, all still with their sand-coloured camouflage, so it was clear that our country was ill-prepared for the conflict.

The liner 'Pasteur' was also anchored at Brest having completed her trials. She eventually sailed to a home port where she did good service, carrying troops between England and America.

After we had tied up a number of troops came aboard, together with their Officers who were clearly not used to seamanship. Fortunately some of the soldiers were old sweats and had worked ships before. I managed to sort out gangs for each hatch and we commenced discharging using our heavy gear.

Pushing the lorries onto the nets was very difficult; regulations stated that all batteries had to be disconnected during transit. To overcome this, I told some drivers to go around reconnecting all batteries so the vehicles could be driven onto the wheel nets; this speeded up the operation. As soon as the vehicles were landed they were driven off to an assembly point. Our drivers had not been told to drive on the right, so you can imagine how many crashes and near misses occurred in those early days.

I found out that a ship with food should have arrived, but due to the mess-up it hadn't. Insofar as was possible our catering staff cooked as much as they could, giving all the foodstuffs we could spare to the troops.

The troops had to sleep in the sheds, as no camp had been organised. What a mess! They had no washing facilities or toilets, using buckets instead. During all this, there was not a Frenchman to be seen on the docks.

When night fell all work had to stop. As no lights could be used, hoisting heavy lorries would be far too dangerous for everyone. We walked up to the town at nightfall, ending up in the *Café de la Paix* in the town square, drinking beer and Pernod. We would return in high spirits, sleep well and awake to another long day's work.

Towards the end of October 1939, after two trips to Brest, we went to London to load for the Far East again. As submarines were not yet a serious threat we had no escort, but luckily nothing untoward happened.

We were now equipped with a gun fitted on the stern that was unable to fire forward of the beam, as required by the Geneva Convention. This was to be manned by DEMS [Defensively Equipped Merchant Ships] gunners who were mainly Naval Reserve personnel: in our case a Sergeant of Marines who had retired only six months earlier and who was calling Adolf Hitler anything but a gentleman. He was, however, extremely good at his job and soon the gunners were becoming expert at loading, etc.

Due to the fact that ships officers were experienced at estimating distances, an officer was always designated as Gunnery Officer. In our case it was the Second Officer, by the name of *Jacques*, who came from London and with whom I got on very well. We had numerous gun practices, but luckily during this period never had to fire in self-defence.

It was the Ship's Officer who called out ranges and gave the order to fire, although according to Marine Law he was a civilian and if injured would be treated as such. In contrast a Navy Sailor, if injured, would receive a pension. How unfair this all was. We were a happy crew, however, and there was no friction of any kind.

It was during this voyage that, while loading at Manila, I slipped on the ladder of number-one hold, landing on a pile of hatch covers. I found that I had strained myself badly and had sustained a hernia. On arrival in Singapore, I went to the Naval Hospital where they fitted me with a support so that I could manage to return home. We returned through the Suez Canal again, but from Gibraltar onward we had to sail in convoy, our first experience of this.

It was during this period that we were receiving news of Dunkerque and the evacuation. So portents were not good. We were glad to arrive safely at Victoria Docks in London where I signed off on 20th February 1940 in order to go home for surgery in Bridgend. A spell of convalescence followed during which my inactivity was hard to bear, for one could not avoid hearing the news, all of which was bad at that moment in time.

Eventually the doctor for the Ministry of Transport decreed that I was fit for light duties, much to the indignation of my own physician. My new duties were to 'stand by' ships in Liverpool. [The term 'stand by' refers to watching over a ship when she is in port, to make sure everything is all right; the individual assigned to stand by is not signed on the ship as a member of the crew although he sleeps and eats, etc on board.] Unfortunately my arrival coincided with the Liverpool Blitz, a full week's night-time of hell…

Rank's mill was blazing and thousands of incendiaries were falling. The ship I was standing by had a cargo of ammunition, so when incendiaries fell on the hatches they had to be quickly removed with shovels. During one night's heavy bombing I observed what looked like a telephone kiosk suspended on a parachute, passing overhead and disappearing behind the cargo sheds. Then there was a tremendous bang and all the shed doors flew out and were leaning on the ship.

I was eventually able to leave the ship to visit my wife who was staying with a relative at West Kirby, but was confronted by a scene of terrible devastation: all the rows of houses running from the docks to the main road had been flattened, not one was left standing, and gas was escaping all over the place.

I saw an Army officer sitting at a trestle table and asked him if there was any possibility of getting around. He said, "You will have to do the best you can, but whatever you do, don't smoke or have a light of any kind." Just then two soldiers came along with two teenaged lads ; they informed the officer that they had caught the boys looting. All he said in response was, "You know what to do, I don't want to know", and I saw the soldiers take these two lads out of sight of the officer and bash them with their rifle butts until they could hardly crawl. Eventually, with the help of a kind motorist, I managed to arrive at my wife's lodgings where I found her in bed after having passed another night in the shelter.

Another problem prevalent at this time was that bombs had also been dropped on the docks, so ships could not be moved until the docks were swept and declared clear. On one jetty a time bomb had fallen between the rails. The only indication of it was a small crater, so an empty railway truck was placed over the hole in case anyone fell in. At about 11 a.m. there was a bang and we could see the truck sailing through the air, going over the warehouses as though it had wings.

Liverpool was a mess, but miracles were done: trams were kept running and people carried on working. I learned that during this period there were six ships, all loading ammunition, on both sides of the river. Liverpool and Birkenhead people believed that these had been the targets but, somehow, not one was hit and even the docks escaped widespread damage.

I soon received a fitness test and passed ready for duty. The Company told me to board the TSS Nestor as Third Officer.

8. Innocents Sent to Safety

The TSS Nestor was a full passenger liner with accommodation on two decks for over a hundred passengers, as well as capacity for over twenty-five thousand tons of cargo. She was a comparatively old ship, a coal burner. I later learned that she consumed about one hundred tons of coal per day, thus requiring a large number of stokers. She had twin, triple-expansion engines and two propellers. Although by no means fast, she was a comfortable ship. Her saloon had a large dome of coloured glass, depicting English and Australian flora, whilst the walls displayed a British coat of arms on one side and the Australian arms on the other, for during peacetime she had been on the Australian run via the Cape. The 'Nestor' had been a beautiful ship in her day, but now she was the usual light grey from top to bottom.

We loaded a small amount of cargo and some twenty passengers, South Africans and Australians, returning home due to the hostilities. Leaving the jetty, we anchored in the centre of the river. We had orders to rig companionways and, much to our amazement, boats full of children of all ages came alongside.

We were told that the Government was promoting the policy that children from large cities, particularly those targeted by enemy action, should be sent to the Colonies in case we were invaded. This scheme had got under way some time earlier, but had been suspended when the liner, 'City of

Benares', had been torpedoed on her way to Canada, with the tragic loss of a number of children. Now it had been decided to resume the operation.

We helped all sixty-five children up the ladders and assisted them with their luggage. They were terribly excited, for they had never dreamed that they would travel the world. Nevertheless, this was so completely new for them that one or two were in tears. When their accommodation had all been assigned, the boys' cabins were on the port side and the girls' to starboard (for their ages varied from six to sixteen years and some girls were clearly young ladies). They were accompanied by a number of escorts, mainly teachers, who were assigned responsibility for so many each.

Our first duties were to reassure the children, show them how lifebelts were fitted and which lifeboats were assigned to them. The passengers assisted us, so that everything was geared to the welfare of our charges.

We left Liverpool on 23rd August 1940, meeting other ships with whom we sailed in convoy via the North Channel, as the St George's Channel had been closed by minefields. We held meetings with the escorts and, as we had two Captains, the Staff Captain took over, allowing the Senior Master and ourselves, the four Officers, to concentrate on manning the bridge. All the foregoing meant that we had various duties over and above our eight hours on bridge watch, often having only a few hours in which to eat and sleep. Fortunately we had our own mess room, with a lift direct to the kitchens.

We were also a designated ship for continuous wireless watch and had three operators who did four hours on and eight off, day and night, continuously. I remember that one day in the mess room one of the operators said to me, "Tubby, I don't feel well". He then fainted, and I sent for the doctor. The doctor brought him round, examined him and came to the conclusion that his fainting was due to a lack of exercise and fresh air. I would never have imagined that this could occur, but it appears that after being in the radio cabin with closed doors for many hours, he had gone straight to his own cabin. As a result, he was now ordered to walk the decks for at least an hour each day.

Altogether we had a complement of more than seventy crew, with sixteen engineers and many firemen, for the boilers burnt coal at a great rate. The catering staff did a wonderful job and everything was soon organised into a routine. During the cold weather the escorts commenced lessons, so that the children understood that this was merely an extension to their education. When the weather improved classes were held on the hatches, boys forward and girls aft. I was deeply impressed, it was just like a travelling school!

We had two nurses on board, and I particularly remember that Saturday morning was 'caster oil morning'. It was amusing to watch the children being rounded up and forced past the nurses who were waiting with large bottles and dessert spoons. None of the children could escape this, even though some protested that they were too old for it, to no avail.

The escorts arranged that the older girls should be encouraged to 'adopt an officer' who would explain how a ship was run and his duties. This was in an effort to discourage the girls' interest in the boys. One such young lady whom I remember well was Miss Pamela O'Dowd who came from

Surbiton and was going to Newcastle in Eastern Australia to stay with relatives.

We sailed in convoy to West Africa and were all relieved that, so far, nothing untoward had happened. However, instead of entering Freetown as planned, we were ordered to Takoradi and told to anchor off the port.

Once we arrived in Takoradi, a boat came alongside laden with boxes, each measuring about 24 by 30 inches, sealed and under guard. As we began to load these into our strongroom, one box was accidentally dropped and I observed two ingots of gold, shaped like house bricks. Before the box was resealed, the gold bricks had to be re-weighed by those in charge in order to confirm that no gold had been scraped off.

We also picked up two European ladies who were almost certainly pregnant, for it was usual for ladies in this condition either to be sent home or to South Africa to a cooler climate and better medical facilities.

We left for Cape Town without an escort. This made us worry, as we had all these young lives aboard. We could rely on our wireless for warnings of danger, but had to keep radio silence unless in an emergency.

We had a safe passage and arrived in Cape Town where the children were allowed to have a run ashore. The South Africans were wonderful to them and kept them entertained until we had finished replenishing our water supplies and fresh foodstuffs.

From Cape Town we proceeded to Durban for fuel and tied up at the Bluff where the children and passengers were taken ashore for the day in order to avoid the dust of bunkering. The work of tipping truck after truck of coal into the bunker hatchways was done as quickly as possible by black South Africans who, I was informed, were prisoners serving time for various offences (but I suggest that they were being used as cheap labour). When bunkering was completed all deck hands were put to work cleaning up the decks ready for the children and the few remaining passengers to return.

Before leaving port we heard over the wireless that the German pocket battleship, 'The Admiral Graf Spee', was on the loose. Commanded by Hans Langsdorrf, this 10,000-ton vessel's six eleven-inch guns, 26 knot speed and armour plating, had captured or sunk many Allied ships in the Atlantic. Now she was believed to be proceeding towards the Indian Ocean to catch ships on the East Africa run. This intelligence was of great concern to us. The vision of children in lifeboats was something we all dreaded, as they would not be able to withstand the harsh conditions, especially in the Southern Hemisphere.

We received new orders and, instead of leaving Durban and sailing East for Australia, we were told to sail South. We sailed southward, the climate becoming progressively cooler, until we were able to see the reflection of the Antarctic ice. The children were amazed by the extremely cold conditions so soon after the warm tropics they had enjoyed, but we kept the real reason for our change of course from them. When they spotted their first whales this gave them something new to think about and also provided their escort-teachers with a new subject for lessons.

We finally headed North again for Freemantle, Western Australia, where about six of the children were met by their relatives or by people willing to foster a child. In Freemantle I managed to have a day off, as I wanted to find my Great Aunt. She had left Rotherfield Peppard at the turn of the century in order to work as a nurse in the Australian gold fields and had married a Swedish sailor who had jumped ship to go to the gold fields, by the name of Christianson. To cut a long story short, I was very lucky indeed to find her living in Dangin, out in the bush some ten miles north of Perth, where I was welcomed with open arms.

After bidding farewell to my Great Aunt I managed to find my way back to the ship and we sailed for Melbourne by night, showing no lights as usual, as the Japanese were now becoming active. We safely docked at dawn and a few more children were met. One girl of about fifteen years of age was met by a nice couple and taken off in their car. I remember thinking that she would be all right, for he was the manager of the Melbourne Power Station and they had no children of their own.

I had assured my Great Aunt that I would try to see my cousin, Walter Butler, who had emigrated to Australia in the late Twenties and was in the Army in Melbourne. I therefore requested a few hours off, put on my full uniform with my ribbons and found the entrance to his army barracks in Arrow Park.

I told my cousin's Commanding Officer that the last time my cousin and I had seen each other I had been only a little boy, so he would be unlikely to recognise me. He gave orders for him to come to his office and, when Wally presented himself, said "Private Butler, meet your cousin from England". I thought Wally was going to fall over, as he clearly though he had been summoned for some misdemeanour.

The C.O. ordered that my cousin should have a day's pass and wished us a happy day together. We enjoyed ourselves thoroughly, parting later that day in a very happy state. Since then I have never heard about Wally or if he survived the War, but would certainly like to find out what happened to him.

We were due to leave Melbourne for Sydney, but were told to delay our sailing as a ship had struck a mine whilst approaching the harbour entrance. It transpired that a Japanese ship flying a neutral flag had laid these mines the previous night. Fortunately, the matter was quickly resolved and we sailed. We were informed later that the Japanese ship involved had been located and sunk.

We berthed at the 'Circular Quay', the main passenger quay, close to the Sydney Harbour Bridge. The Australian Press had come on board in full force, taking photographs of all and sundry, as the largest contingent of our remaining children was due to disembark. One reporter commented "These are the kind of children we have been hoping for." He was entirely right, for they were well behaved and a credit to their parents.

The local authorities, the escorts and those who were waiting to claim the children were busy all day, arranging where the children should go. Suddenly the tears started to flow, for now it hit the children that we were the last link in the chain that connected them to home; many had no idea of what the future held, and from here on they would be alone.

The children's escorts also left us in Sydney. I understand that they were given a short respite before being sent home via the Pacific Ocean to the United States, from whence they were to be flown home. I was later told that the ship they were on was sunk by a Japanese submarine and that the female escorts were held on an island, whilst the male escorts were taken to Japan. This report was, however, only hearsay and I have never been able to confirm it.

Our cargo of gold had been discharged in Sydney and I learned later that it was destined for America to help in the Lend Lease Agreement.

Once everything was settled we left Sydney for Newcastle, to take on a full load of bunker coal, and it was here that young Pamela O'Dowd would disembark to join her new family.

We returned to Sydney to load cargo for our voyage home and were greatly heartened to learn that the 'Graf Spee' had been scuttled off Montevideo. Nevertheless, even as the threat of the 'Graf Spee' was lifted, the U-boat menace was increasing.

On our return journey, we called at Melbourne once more, where further large quantities of various items were loaded. To my surprise a chauffeur-driven car drew up to the wharf. When the door was opened, out stepped Miss Pamela O'Dowd as though she had done it all her life. She had come to see us, to relate that her new family was very kind, that she was happy and would shortly be enrolling in the best college in Melbourne.

Leaving Melbourne, we sailed across the Great Australian Bight to Albany in the extreme South West of the country. As we approached no harbour could be seen, but suddenly an entrance was observed between the hills. Inside there was a completely land-locked harbour, in the middle of which lay an ancient hulk of a sailing ship. The pilot told us to secure alongside it.

This part of Australia was apparently the principal fruit growing area and hundreds of boxes of apples were loaded into our cool chambers. The owner of this consignment came on board to see the operation himself, as his livelihood depended on its safe delivery.

Our next port of call was Durban, to continue loading, and then Cape Town where loading was completed. Our cargo included thousands of boxes of tinned fruit and jam, etc, all of which were products for which South Africa was noted. The people we encountered there certainly seemed to be very pro-British and were doing their utmost to assist the war effort.

From South Africa we sailed across the South Atlantic to join up with other ships from South America. We proceeded up the coast of Brazil keeping close inshore in shallow water, where submarines would find it difficult to attack us. As we passed the mouth of the Amazon we observed that the water was brown with sediment carried by the current, even though we were well out of sight of land. Suddenly a ship in the middle of the convoy hoisted two vertical black balls and blew her whistle to attract attention. She was full of iron ore and had a deep draught, causing her to hit a sandbank and stop. We had to proceed on our way but, luckily, when the tide rose she managed to free herself and joined us the next day.

We eventually arrived back in Glasgow on the 8th February 1941, and I was able to go home for a few days.

9. A Second Year of War Service

I had been on leave in Bridgend only a short time when I was asked to report back for duty and assigned to stand by a Company vessel in Birkenhead Docks. My principal job would be to prevent any looting, as the ship in question had sunk and was resting on the dock bottom. A bomb had struck her without exploding, but had penetrated her cargo and hull and flooded the hold. This had been enough to sink her.

The stricken ship was full of Army supplies, including thousands of pairs of army boots and uniforms of various kinds. These would be recovered as soon as possible and the ship salvaged, but conditions prevailing at the time were delaying the undertaking. I stood by the ship for two weeks and was then ordered to go to Glasgow.

My orders were to join the 'Euryades' that was being prepared for sea. On arrival at the port I found out that she had been destined for the scrap yard but, as she could still float and her engine was found to be in working order, she had to be commissioned.

The 'Euryades' had been built in 1914 and was a coal-burning, 'open-bottomed' ship, meaning that she had no double bottom for water ballast to keep her upright. She had an extremely tall funnel and, as she had no fans to force the wind up through this funnel, was run on what is called 'natural draught' and the wind had to be relied on to do all the work.

Due to her design she could not now go to sea without some weight in the bottom, so we loaded whatever cargo was available. We then sailed to Liverpool to take on more, until we had sufficient cargo for the purpose. We anchored off the Mersey to await the arrival of other ships from the Bristol Channel to make up our convoy for the voyage to Halifax, Nova Scotia, via the Northern Channel.

Our escort consisted of a light cruiser, namely HMS Hawkins, a destroyer and Corvettes. The latter were small oil-burning boats, their hulls similar in design to those of deep-sea trawlers. They were fitted with a small cannon, machine guns and depth charges and, when a heavy swell was running, would disappear from sight as each swell passed.

I met some of the Officers of these Corvettes who stated that they found their boats dry, but so buoyant that they rolled excessively. Their meals usually had to be eaten sitting on the floor, whilst their bunks had canvas edges to stop their occupants from rolling out. I reckon that the cooks on these craft were heroes for, although the galleys were frequently ankle-deep in water, meals were produced no matter what happened.

One night whilst I was on the bridge there was a sudden flash as a ship in the far column was torpedoed. We carried on, as instructed, while the rescue vessel at the back of the convoy proceeded to the spot to look for survivors.

A few nights later at about 11 p.m. we were proceeding at our usual seven knots when I observed a white glow dead ahead. Gradually a very large iceberg appeared, lit up by the destroyer's searchlight. I had to alter course around this, bearing in mind that there was another ship close on my port beam in the middle column. As we passed the berg, one could smell it. I found out later that the odour was the result of whales rubbing themselves on the berg to rid themselves of sea lice.

We eventually arrived in Halifax without further incident and went alongside, where our cargo was discharged and the loading began. What I was unaware of was that my wife had written to her uncle in New York to tell him I would be arriving in Halifax and, to my surprise, he turned up. Unfortunately I could not invite him aboard due to strict security, but we had a pleasant few hours together in the town and it was most kind of him to travel all that way.

Our cargo consisted of cases of foodstuffs and equipment and, when the holds were full, three tiers of enormous cases were put on the decks, fore and aft, over the hatches. These contained lorry parts that would be assembled when we reached our destination.

As we proceeded South in convoy, further ships from New York joined us and then others, from Chesapeake Bay, making a sizeable convoy with a very heavy escort. We again hugged the shoreline, as U-boats were quite active off the American coast at that time.

Continuing South, we passed the West Indies and once we were off Pernambuco the convoy dispersed. Some ships were bound for South America, but the 'Euryades' sailed direct to South Africa without calling anywhere.

We rounded the Cape of Good Hope and went up the East African coast into the Red Sea, via the Gulf of Aden. During this passage the helmsmen had considerable difficulty in steering the ship, as the tiers of cases on our decks were high and acted like a sail. The helmsmen were therefore put on hourly watches instead of two-hour watches to avoid fatigue.

We arrived at Suez and commenced unloading our deck cargo into barges until nightfall. One night, when all work had ceased and we were relaxing, suddenly all hell was let loose. German planes approached us, showing full lights, and were taken for friendly aircraft until the bombs started to drop. We quickly manned our machine guns and our DEMS gunners began firing the Bofors from the aft of our ship. The enemy planes now extinguished their lights and came in with their engines shut off until right above us, so we were firing blind but hoping to put them off their aim.

Bombs dropped on both sides of our ship, but I saw that one had hit the liner, MV Georgic, aft of her passenger accommodation. Twenty minutes or so after the raid had ended flames were observed coming from the stricken liner and we could see people jumping into the water. We lowered one of our lifeboats, of which I took charge, rowed towards the 'Georgic' and were able to pick some people up. In the meantime her anchor had been slipped and she was steaming towards the beach. The engine room staff were jumping out of a door in the hull, so we followed in her wake until the tug arrived and took off all the crew we had picked up. The 'Georgic' was now one great mass of flames, her forced draught ventilation having been left on causing the fire to spread, and nothing could be done to assist her.

I found out later that the 'Georgic' had been towed into Bombay where she had been rebuilt and put into service again.

Included at the end of this Chapter is a reproduction of my official Report to the Company on the above incident, submitted by me to the Company Office on 8th December 1941.

Once all our cargo had been discharged we sailed down the Red Sea, bound for Aden, but had to anchor off the port as there was no space available for us. After waiting at anchor for a couple of weeks we entered the port to load ballast before proceeding into the Indian Ocean, as the monsoon was at its height and heavy seas would be encountered. Truckloads of stones and rubble were put into the bottom of the holds. We then left port and sailed South for Mombassa.

The usual problems ensued at Mombassa, for all the wharfs were occupied and we had to tie up in the middle of a creek off the main channel. We were there for a couple of weeks and were beginning to feel rather fed up and isolated, so I gained permission to use the 'Jolly Boat' [a heavy clinker-built utility boat with a square transom, about eighteen feet long]. I equipped her with a set of sails out of a lifeboat, but this made her over-canvassed so I put two bags of sand in the bottom. We had good fun with her and explored a wide area.

One day I was walking up a path through the trees and stopped to admire a clearing planted with pineapples. Suddenly a voice behind me said "Would you like one?" and as I gratefully replied in the affirmative, the middle-aged Kenyan gentleman who had addressed me in perfect English cut one, prepared it and gave it to me. It was nectar, full of juice, and we sat down and talked about all manner of things. It transpired that my companion knew Cardiff better than I did, for he had served on ships from South Wales and had lived in a road off Bute Street not far from where Shirley Bassey was born. He had returned to Mombassa when he had saved enough money, bought a plot of land and married, living a peaceful and comfortable existence, growing everything they needed and keeping chickens.

When we were finally allocated a wharf and our ballast was discharged, various items were loaded in the lower hold. I remember that a local shopkeeper came out to ask if we would take a few parcels of goods to his store at our next port, and this we agreed to do.

We sailed for a small place called Tanga to load 'sisal'. This had become an important cargo, as Manila, which produced hemp, had been lost to the Japanese. Although sisal was not a totally satisfactory substitute, it was needed for the manufacture of ships' ropes. I had little experience of ropes made of this fibre and found it terrible for bending around bollards, etc. but it was all that was available at that time.

The residents of Tanga were very glad to see us. They had a large crop of sisal, but shipping it was a problem and our arrival in port was most welcome. They were so pleased that they gave all the crew a party out on a large lawn. What interested us particularly were the surrounding trees, some festooned with what appeared to be large cucumbers (loofahs) and others covered with the most wonderful flowers.

Hundreds of bales of sisal were loaded in the lower holds, sufficient to act as ballast for our next stage. We left Tanga, sailing further south to Beira in Portuguese East Africa to load

Rhodesian Copper, an important metal used in armaments, etc.

On arrival at Beira it became evident that the Rhodesian Copper could not be placed on top of the large bales of sisal already in the holds, as the substantial weight of the ingots would raise the ship's centre of gravity to a critical level. It was therefore decided to unload the sisal onto the wharf, load the copper into the bottom of the holds and reload the sisal on top of the cargo of copper.

Leaving Beira, our next port of call was Durban, to bunker, for we were running low and this was the last opportunity to obtain coal before reaching home. After refuelling, we rounded the Cape of Good Hope for Cape Town where thousands of cases of canned fruit and meat were loaded. Cases were even broken open, so that a few more tins could be pushed in between the hatch beams. Some cabins lay empty, so these were also filled. The South Africans were furnishing substantial assistance to the war effort, not only by supplying essential goods, but also troops for the North African campaign.

We joined up with a couple of other ships and sailed for Sierra Leone, to meet other ships homeward bound. We were having problems with the ship's steering on this passage, being unable to put the helm hard over either way. On arrival at the port the local Lloyds Surveyor came on board to look into the problem. I immediately recognised him as a Chief Officer of the SS Nohata, from my apprenticeship days. He said he felt very lucky to have landed his job and that he had been in Freetown for nearly a year.

During the examination and manipulation of the steering gear it was found that the quadrant had dropped nearly an inch and jammed, so further investigations were needed to find the cause.

The quadrant is a large piece of gear, forming one-quarter of a circle, which is attached at its centre to the top of the rudder post. Rudder chains are attached to the outer edge and these pull the quadrant from side to side, thus moving the rudder to port and starboard as required.

A diver eventually came out from the Naval Station and went down to examine the base of the rudder. He found that the circular piece of metal in the lower connection, on which the weight of the rudder rested, had broken and had allowed the rudder to fall. As nothing could be done there to remedy the problem, we sailed with a fully laden ship, but were put at the end of a column. This was to give us more room to manoeuvre, although we had instructions not to put the helm hard over either way.

To give a better idea of the parlous and aged condition of our ship, it was during our last passage from South Africa that the Chief Officer had told the Bos'n to smarten up some of the deck houses and give them a coat of paint. When the crew started to scrape off the rust, they quickly had to stop, for it was found that rust had eaten right through the metal and thick paper had been put over the holes and then painted over.

I had also noted that there was a peculiar, musty smell in my cabin that no amount of cleaning could remove. On further examination I concluded that there must be something stored in a space under my settee, but no door was apparent. I scraped paint away and found a foot-square door that had been painted over for years. In the bottom of the space lay some old newspapers that had been the source of the musty odour. To my surprise, these were all dated 1916, two years after the outbreak of the First World War, creating an interesting parallel with our own situation.

We left Freetown in convoy with a heavy escort and proceeded North, keeping well out to the centre of the Atlantic. It was then that the Commander in charge of the convoy gave the order that we were to reverse course 180 degrees and proceed back on our course. This we duly did and, after about four days, the order came to return to our original northerly course. Only then did we find out that the German pocket battleship, 'The Bismark', had sunk HMS Hood and had also attacked a convoy ahead of us. She had been followed, however, and after great efforts by our men-of-war and aircraft she was finally stopped, and sunk.

We arrived home to Liverpool at last, having taken six weeks on this passage instead of the usual three.

On the following pages is the report of action, as submitted to the Company Office of Alfred Holt & Company in Liverpool by 3rd Officer Ron W Tubb:

S/S EURYADES, 8TH DECEMBER 1941
Re:- ATTACK BY HOSTILE AIRCRAFT ON SHIPS AT SUEZ 13.07.41

The 'EURYADES' had been at anchor in Suez Bay for a matter of three weeks, during which time a number of Air Raids had been experienced. During these Raids, Bombs and Land Mines were dropped from a great height and all near the Canal. On the night of July 13th we were anchored in a position about due East of Atakah and South of South West Beacon, with the S/S Almanzora anchored 1,000 yards East of us, and the M/V Georgic a further 1,000 yards away and in line with the 'Almanzora' and both just abaft of our starboard beam.

The night was cloudy, with bright moonlight and a light northerly breeze. At 11.45 pm the 'Air Raid' sirens were sounded from Suez and destroyers anchored in the bay. We were on anchor watches and I (as Third Officer), on hearing the sirens, called all Gun Crews, the Chief Officers and the Master to their stations.

The Anti-Aircraft armament consisted of a Bofors on the poop, two stripped Lewis, one on each side of the Boat Deck and two Hotchkiss, one on each Bridge Wing. All the Gun Crews were at their stations, myself manning the starboard bridge machine gun.

About twenty minutes after the sounding of the sirens, I observed a plane approaching from the West, about five hundred feet up and quite close. The plane was showing full navigation lights and we took it for a British plane searching for the enemy. It passed directly over our bow and soon after we saw a bomb explode about 100 feet ahead of the 'Georgic'. We at once knew the plane to be hostile and realised how we had been tricked. It was obviously the German Pilot's ruse to make us think it was a British plane and it proved successful, as not a single shot was fired at the plane by any ship or shore battery. We at once ordered all the Gun Crews to fire at any plane, whether with or without lights if seen approaching from any direction, without further orders.

Soon after the first attack another plane was heard approaching from the West, but was not seen by anyone aboard our vessel and no shots were fired, as the plane's direction could not be determined. One bomb was dropped in this attack and exploded off the starboard bow of the 'Georgic'.

Soon afterwards, another plane was heard approaching from the West and I managed to observe it passing the stars and immediately opened fire, and three quarters of a belt went out. I observed tracers passing close to the enemy plane, but could not discern anything more. No other shots were fired at this plane and two bombs were dropped, one close under the counter of the 'Almanzora' and the other hitting the 'Georgic' at the after end of the promenade deck. Soon afterwards another plane came in from the West, dropping two bombs near American vessels anchored at Atakah, and it passed over us. Although not seen by anyone, the Bofors crew fired off a number of rounds at the plane's sound. Then a bomb fell midway between the 'Euryades' and the 'Almanzora'. This wide aiming was probably due to the result of our Bofors fire.

We waited for more attacks, but none came. Then a signal was read being flashed from the bridge of the 'Georgic' asking for boats to be sent, and this was replied to. Meanwhile the damaged vessel was seen to be on fire, the flames rapidly spreading fore and aft, so the Master ordered me to take number four boat to the assistance of the vessel, which duty I carried out. My crew consisting of a Senior Midshipman, First and Second Stewards and five of the Chinese crew.

We observed now that the 'Georgic' was under way and steaming fast in the direction of the North Beacon, so we rowed in her wake searching as we went. We returned at 6 am, together with boats number five and six, in the charge of our Second Officer and an extra Third Officer.

All persons aboard the 'Euryades' were excellent during the raid, but feelings ran high about having been deceived in the first instance and we determined never to let it happen again.

Report submitted by
Ron W Tubb 3rd Officer 'Euryades'

10. Further Experience of War

I went home for a much-needed leave and arrived unexpectedly, to be greeted by my wife who immediately burst into tears. She had known that I was homeward bound and, having heard on the wireless of the number of ships sunk by the 'Bismark', had become very worried about my safety.

On this leave I was having trouble again with the injury I had sustained on the 'Glengarry' and found that I would have to enter hospital again to rectify the problem. Fortunately the hospital was only a short distance from home. I found myself in a ward with various war casualties: some with limbs missing, others with bullet wounds, etc and two of us scheduled for abdominal surgery.

The nurses were simply wonderful and nothing was too much trouble, although some looked tired out with the long hours on duty. There was a side ward off ours and in it were two German officers from Highland Farm on the outskirts of Bridgend. This had been turned into a Prisoner of War camp for German Generals and other high-ranking prisoners. A British soldier was always on duty at the door leading into our ward, with orders that if either German tried to enter he was to be restrained, or killed if anyone was attacked.

A period of recovery followed, during which I returned to the Nautical College and sat my Master Mariner's examination, passing it on 1st July 1942. The Ministry of Transport passed me fit for further duties, so I reported back to Liverpool for my next assignment. So many ships had been sunk and people lost that Navigating Officers and Captains with experience were urgently needed. I hoped for promotion in due course.

I was assigned to a ship lying on the Birkenhead side of the river and, from the work being carried out on her, I knew that she was bound for a Northern Convoy to Murmansk. This made me feel very apprehensive, as I knew the perils of this run. I did not mention the matter to my wife, so as to spare her more worry.

After standing by this ship for a couple of days the Super from the Company Office came aboard. He asked me whether I had unpacked my gear which, luckily, was still in my cases. He told me to grab it all and come with him in a taxi. We went through the Mersey Tunnel and I completed forms to serve as Third Officer on another Company ship, called the 'Antenor'. As we approached the quay I could see hundreds of troops boarding her. Noticing that they were not wearing winter gear, I assumed that we would be heading South.

This ship was similar in several respects to the TSS Nestor. Her three 'tween decks had been fitted with rows of wooden bunks for the troops and a line of wooden latrines on the port side of both fore and aft decks, whilst their Officers were assigned to the passenger accommodation. Hatchways had been fitted with exit steps and curtains that could be opened in such as way as to prevent any light being observed on entry and exit.

Informed that the Far East would be our destination, the Captain, Second Officer and myself attended a Convoy

Meeting on the day before sailing in the Liver Building that housed Naval Personnel in charge of all shipping movements. We were advised that, due to the importance of the convoy which would consist of a large number of passenger lines containing thousands of troops, all Allied aircraft had been instructed not to approach within one mile of us. If they did so, we were instructed to open fire no matter what, without waiting for orders.

All told, there were about fourteen ships, as more joined us from the Clyde. We proceeded through the North Channel with an unusually heavy escort that included a light cruiser, two destroyers and Corvettes. Our speed was to be twelve knots, the fastest convoy I had ever been in, so we were looking forward to a quick passage.

When we approached the north coast of Ireland the weather was overcast, with low cloud and light rain that impaired visibility, so a sharp lookout was the order of the day. Suddenly we heard an aircraft overhead, circling the convoy continuously. All our guns were following its course when all at once it broke through the clouds, almost overhead. Every ship opened fire and we saw that the aircraft received a direct hit. We recognised immediately that it was a Sunderland Flying Boat. A destroyer immediately rushed to the area.

We were all very upset by this incident. The Senior Officer on the cruiser must have understood our dismay, as a destroyer was sent through all the lines to inform us over a loudspeaker that we had acted correctly, the pilot had not obeyed instructions and, if it happened again, we would know what to do.

The Commanding Officer, his Adjutant, the Captain and Officers held a conference to discuss various matters, including identifying any jobs that the troops could assist with, as idle hands were bad for morale and a source of worry. As a result, a number of new duties for the troops were identified.

Firstly, we arranged for machineguns to be mounted on the boat deck, to be manned day and night. Secondly, a guard would be posted at the exit of each hatch to watch for anyone smoking, as the latrines on deck were in use day and night and a glowing cigarette-end could have been seen for miles in the darkness.

Finally, the many Engineers amongst the troops were formed into two gangs, one port and one starboard, to work on improving the condition of the ship's life-saving equipment.

The equipment included four motor lifeboats and a number of mechanically propelled boats; the latter were useless for any distance and could only be used to propel one clear of a sinking ship. These were equipped with a number of levers that had to be pulled back and forth to turn a propeller. The rods, which had had little or no maintenance, were corroded and were not functioning correctly.

To encourage competition between the two gangs, strict orders were given that only one boat on each side was to be worked on at any one time. The men descended many times to the engine room, to borrow all the tools and equipment they needed. As each boat was completed, it was my duty to examine it. If the job had been done satisfactorily, pulling only one lever made all the others operate and the propeller turn without any effort. I would then give my verdict to the teams.

The Adjutant who was a Colonel and a holder of the Victoria Cross was an example to everyone in fulfilling his responsibilities and, particularly, in handling the troops. I well remember one particular occasion when he raised everyone's morale in the following manner...

Our saloon had been stripped of most of its luxury, but the grand piano had been left. The Adjutant asked whether anyone could play it and a Lance Corporal volunteered modestly that he played a bit, so was asked to 'have a go'. Suddenly, to everyone's amazement, the saloon was filled with the most wonderful sound of classical music. After about half an hour he changed tempo and embarked on a selection of modern numbers, delighting us all. (I found out later that he was a concert pianist in civilian life.) The troops were then asked if anyone else had a musical instrument. At first no-one wanted to admit to having brought an instrument on board, as Army Regulations forbade troops from carrying any excess equipment. The Adjutant, however, told them that no action would be taken against them, so a clarinet, a trumpet and a couple of other instruments were produced. On that occasion and on many others we enjoyed some wonderful musical evenings.

The Commanding Officer entered into the spirit of the thing, asking whether anyone else had something to add to the occasion. One of the troops stated he was a cartoonist and, using a board and chalk, did some wonderful caricatures of the C.O., the Adjutant and of our Captain. Captain Kelly was quite short and rotund, so the caricature produced raised loud and appreciative laughter.

In the middle of the convoy was an Elder & Fyffe ship carrying female nursing personnel and others who were going to Army hospitals. As the weather became warmer the young ladies could be observed in bathing costumes enjoying the sun. I believe that most troop ships listed as the boys ran to port or starboard to look at them, all wishing.

We eventually arrived in Cape Town and, on the first day, all troops were ordered to do a route march to exercise their limbs. As they marched through the town, local young ladies pushed oranges, cigarettes, etc into their tunics, giving them a great welcome. That evening they were allowed ashore, with instructions on what not to do and to avoid certain young ladies, for a sick soldier was no good to anyone. Thousands of soldiers descended on the city and, after being confined for so long aboard, they undoubtedly drank every bottle of beer available. All night stragglers were being returned in police vans, those that could still walk helping those who were staggering. The people of Cape Town took it all in their stride, and I admired them for this.

We left Cape Town still under escort, to round the Cape of Good Hope and travel up the east coast of Africa, through the Mozambique Channel. Here one of our ships was diverted to Madagascar, to assist the authorities in suppressing a rebellion that had broken out there.

During this passage our Ships Surgeon phoned the bridge stating that a soldier had acute appendicitis and that he would have to operate. The Army Doctor, who had been a gynaecologist in civilian life, would assist him. When all was ready they phoned the bridge again and we hoisted our pennant to inform all ships that an operation was in progress. It seemed only minutes before the phone rang again stating that all was done, so we resumed our course which had been altered to steady the ship. Later, the troops' Medical Officer stated that he had never seen anything like it, the operation had taken less than ten minutes and only three stitches had been needed. It had clearly been a success, as in a couple of days I saw the soldier in question walking the deck.

We entered the Red Sea again, arriving at Suez where the troops disembarked and their stores were loaded into lighters. This was all carried out as speedily as possible, to avoid the Germans finding out about it and sending aircraft. This operation was undertaken to support the build-up of troops in North Africa and to turn the war around in that arena.

Leaving Suez we received orders to proceed to Bombay, where we arrived safely and began loading various items of cargo. As we had a qualified surgeon, a number of Army and Air Force personnel, Merchant Seamen and civilians, were received aboard. The Forces' personnel were mostly from Burma and had had to leave in order to recover from injuries and fevers. The civilians were a diverse group of refugees from Singapore, including lady secretaries from British companies and nurses from the Singapore Hospital.

The stories I was told by these individuals graphically described the hardship and privation they had undergone. One party had reached Sumatra and had walked from the East Coast to the West Coast, relying on villagers to give them food. Reaching the West Coast they had tried to locate a ship, but found only fishing boats that were useless for a sea passage. After a couple of weeks a British Warship had come down the coast, looking for survivors. They boarded her and sailed to Madras, from whence they had made their way to Bombay.

The Merchant Seamen were from ships that had been torpedoed in the Indian Ocean. Some of them had inhaled fuel oil and were in agony, coughing day and night, and fighting for breath. Others were from a ship laden with iron ore that had split in two and sunk, only ten managing to get into lifeboats.

Leaving Bombay, we proceeded to South Africa where large amounts of cargo were loaded in Durban and Cape Town respectively. Meanwhile, our Surgeon was kept busy with the sick and injured, assisted by the nurses from Singapore.

We then sailed for South America, where ships from the Argentine joined us. Although the waters were thought to be clear of enemy ships, we kept close inshore in shallow water. As we approached the West Indies our escort joined us, together with various tankers from the West Indies and the United States. When the convoy was complete, additional escorts joined, one being an American destroyer with four funnels, of First World War vintage.

When we finally arrived in Liverpool all the troops and passengers left, relieved that it was all over, and I went home for a much needed leave.

11. Life on Seagoing Tankers

After my leave I returned to the Company Office in Liverpool, to be informed that the Ministry of Shipping had asked
whether any officers on the Company Pool would be willing
to transfer to tankers. A number of us agreed and shortly
afterwards I received notification to go to London to visit the
offices of the Shell Shipping Company. After the interview,
which went well, I was told I would shortly be given my
orders. The day was a particularly memorable one, as my wife
was able to accompany me to London.

When my orders arrived they were for me to join the MV
Cymbula at Milford Haven as Third Officer. The manage-
ment of tankers was new to me and I needed to learn all about
their operation.

The 'Cymbula' was at anchor in the middle of the harbour,
awaiting orders. Our crew consisted of European Officers and
Engineers and the remaining crew were Chinese. The Chief
Officer, named Watson and originally from the Shetland Isles,
became a good friend of mine. On my arrival he introduced
me to various items with which I might not be familiar. I
remember in particular some canvas contraptions suspended
from wires between the masts and hanging into the tops of the
tanks. He explained that these were used to cause a draught,
to expel the highly flammable gases that remained in the
tanks after discharging their cargo of fuel.

I also noticed that steam was used to clean any remaining oil from the tanks after discharging the cargo. The water and oil residue from this process would later be pumped ashore, where the oil would be separated and re-used. It is a source of grave concern nowadays that tankers sailing under 'flags of convenience' often clean tanks at sea, to save time in port. They then discharge the waste material directly into the ocean. I believe that ships found guilty of doing this should be heavily fined for the environmental damage caused.

We joined up with ships from Liverpool and Glasgow, with an escort consisting of HMS Hawkins, the same light cruiser that had escorted the 'Euryades', together with two Corvettes and two motor-launches. The launches were wooden boats, one hundred feet long, capable of 14 knots and designated for escort duties only. The principal armaments were a Bofors and depth charges.

All the tankers and ships were in ballast and destined for the West Indies and South America. Once we had passed the Azores, the 'Hawkins' and one Corvette left us to join a homeward-bound convoy, whilst we proceeded South.

One tanker in the convoy was acting as a supply ship and carried a tank of diesel oil. It also had two rows of unprimed depth charges on its upper deck. During a long passage escorts could be refuelled by means of a pipe that trailed over the stern with a rope and buoy attached. The ship in need of oil fuel would approach from astern, using a grappling iron to pick up the rope and a winch to draw the pipe aboard. This was then bolted onto their intake pipe. When the operation was completed the tanker would draw the pipe back aboard until it was required again.

The day after our heavy escorts departed we were attacked by a submarine pack and all hell was let loose. A wing ship was hit, the escorts were dropping depth charges all over the place, and I saw that a Norwegian tanker in the next column was hit but had kept her position and did not sink. When dawn broke, a Corvette came through the lines with German seamen on deck, to show us that it was not all one-sided and to boost our morale.

The escorts had used all their depth charges and these had to be replenished from the supply tanker. This was achieved by the two ships running parallel, with carefully adjusted speed and course, while the depth charges were suspended between them on wires and transferred two at a time. This took most of the day, but it was the only means of doing the operation without stopping the convoy.

The tanker that had been hit never lost her place in the convoy, in spite of having sustained a hole in the side as big as a bus, but would have to go into port for repairs. Tankers when empty had tanks 'open to the sea' which meant that, in the event of such a calamity, a tank could be flooded by opening valves on the opposite side. Thus the ship's list could be compensated for and, using other tanks and their valves, the ship's trim could be adjusted.

We finally left the convoy and proceeded to the island of Curaçao in the Dutch West Indies to load, whilst the other ships headed South to the Argentine to load wheat or, if they were refrigerated, to load meat products.

Curaçao was Dutch owned, and the company Royal Dutch Shell had a massive refinery there to crack the crude oil from Venezuela. Small tankers were used to bring the crude to the island from the Gulf of Maracaibo, as the coastal waters are too shallow for large ships. We proceeded up the channel that divides the capital, Willemstad, passing through the pontoon bridge that had been opened for us.

We began to load 'aviation spirit', known as 100 Octane, and all precautions had to be taken during this operation, as the spirit was highly flammable. While loading, the tank tops were sealed and the wheel valves on the deck were used to open and shut the entry pipes in the bottom of each. Air was expelled through ullage pipes in the main deck and one used a weighted line, like a plumb line, to monitor the rise of the contents. The level was allowed to rise until it was about three feet below its maximum, at which point loading was stopped. The valve was then shut and another, on an empty tank, quickly opened. One had to be extremely quick, for delay meant that petrol would flow everywhere, causing considerable damage. When all tanks were filled to the required level, the pressure was reduced on the shore pumps and the tanks topped off. The ship's trim was adjusted by means of the fore and aft tanks.

We always had oxygen equipment handy. One day, when an apprentice was checking the rise of the petrol in a tank and fumes were coming out of the ullage pipe, I saw him suddenly collapse. I yelled for assistance, as another tank had to be opened quickly whilst I rushed to him with the oxygen and clamped the mask over his face. He quickly revived and had no recollection of what had happened.

Tankers at that time had two fore and aft bulkheads and nine transverse bulkheads. On this tanker that made twenty-seven sections, each completely separate. Loading was achieved by connecting pipes to our tanker from the shore. These led through into the bottoms of various tanks. To unload, we had two pump-rooms, one forward and one aft, each with two pumps, so that we were able to unload without shore assistance. When we were fully loaded the Victualling Officer ensured that all the product had been received and checked.

We sailed for Port of Spain on the island of Trinidad to join other ships with which we would sail in convoy, past Port Guyana, up the Brazilian coast and then disperse to our various destinations. However, while in port we received orders not to sail, as a U-boat was operating in the area. It had attacked the island of Aruba and was believed now to be somewhere near Trinidad. Later we were told that a Dutch man-of-war had hunted down, found and destroyed the U-boat, so now we could proceed.

We sailed in convoy until, in the vicinity of Pernambuco, we left to sail East for Africa. We were informed that when we came within flying distance planes from Africa would be escorting us in, as our cargo was urgently needed. About half way through our voyage we received a wireless message in-structing us to proceed two hundred miles South and resume our easterly course, as a submarine had been detected on our old route. We sailed on, keeping a careful lookout, and finally arrived in Takoradi, in Ghana, and docked safely.

We were to discharge part of our cargo here for the local aerodromes, and the Captain and I reported to Naval Control to register our arrival and receive orders. The Naval Authority asked where we had been. Aircraft had been searching for us and, failing to find our ship, they reported us missing. We told them of the instructions we had received to alter our course and that they had probably been searching further North of us. It was eventually found that there had been a breakdown in communication between Naval Control and Air Control in Freetown, so some heads would be rolling.

Leaving Takoradi, we were instructed to proceed along the coast to a certain point where we would observe a small yellow buoy, about a mile off shore, that was connected to an underwater pipeline. In the Gulf of Guinea the tidal flow was in one direction, from West to East, so when the buoy was sighted we steamed past it, turned and, after again passing it close to seaward, dropped our anchor and dropped back until the buoy was close to our starboard beam. An American in a motor boat approached us from the shore and tied a line to the buoy. We winched this aboard., found the wire and then the hose-end appeared. This pipe was bolted to our midship connection and when that task was completed we signalled to the shore by lamp. When a reply was received, we commenced pumping.

The pressure required was so great that we had to use two pumps on the line, as this aviation spirit was going well inland to tanks in airfields built mainly by the Americans for servicing arriving aircraft. When the tanks were full a further signal was made, to stop pumping. Then the plate was re-bolted onto the end of the pipeline and this was lowered to its original position.

I found out that American-built bomber planes were being flown to Brazil, but as that was a Neutral country they could not be armed and the crews had to dress in civilian clothes. The planes were refuelled in Brazil and then flown to West

Africa where they refuelled again before being flown to the war zone in North Africa.

Next we sailed to Lagos in Nigeria, where our discharging was completed. We tied up to a jetty on the opposite side of the harbour from the city and saw that the buildings nearby were without roofs and looked as though they had been on fire. We were informed that an incident occurred when an earlier tanker was discharging. The tanker in question had discharged petrol in Takoradi earlier, at which time the plate and gasket on the stern pipe had not been properly sealed. In Lagos, as discharge was carried out via the midship pipeline, the condition of the stern pipe had not been noticed.

As luck would have it, an apprentice returning from a run ashore could smell petrol vapour and saw the fuel leaking from the stern line. He rushed aboard, closed the valve and raised the alarm. Tied up astern of the tanker was an old trawler and, somehow, some hot ashes were dumped overboard. The water became a raging fire rushing towards the tanker, but stopped short of it, narrowly avoiding a catastrophe.

Leaving Lagos we sailed West in ballast and were directed to the Chesapeake Bay and to Baltimore. Up to this point we had no idea why, but soon found out. We berthed opposite a Kaiser shipyard where 'Liberty Ships' were being constructed and were boarded by an army of workmen who began to build a girder deck over our main deck, both fore and aft, so that we could carry planes as well as oil.

A representative of Naval Armament came on board to inquire what armament we had. I told him we had two Oerlikons, one each end of the bridge, and a 4.7 on the stern.

He commented that this was not much. A further gang then came aboard to put strengthening girders on our wheel-houses and install Twin Colt Browning machineguns on pedestals. These were point fives and could fire 1,250 rounds per minute; the magazines on each were enormous. Spare ammunition arrived in a lorry and we had difficulty in finding storage space close to the guns.

By now the girder decking was taking shape. Once it was completed, twenty-four fighter-bombers would be loaded, twelve fore and twelve aft, and made secure.

Amidst all this activity, we received a telephone call from our New York office, advising that two of our Chinese crewmen were in jail, and would I go to see if anything could be done. I put on my full uniform and two ribbons and reported to a local Precinct Police Station.

The Sergeant on duty informed me that the two men had gone into a bar to purchase a small bottle of whisky each, while at the same time a radio in the bar was broadcasting a report about the attack on Pearl Harbour. A drunken American, seeing our Chinese, presumed they were Japanese and started a fight, resulting in all three being taken to jail by the Police. I then entered the Court. When our case came up, the Judge asked whether anyone was representing the accused, so I stood up to state who I was and he invited me to the front of the courtroom to explain the situation. The end result was that the Judge ordered my crew members to be released at once and the American to be jailed for 14 days. He further ordered that the American was to be shown photographs, so that in future he would know a Chinese from a Japanese.

The upshot of this incident was that the Chinese crew subsequently made sure I was cared for in every way. The word must have been passed on as, in the future, every Chinese crew treated me in the same manner.

Once the fighter-bombers were loaded and secured, we sailed from Baltimore through the Chesapeake-Delaware Canal on passage towards New York. This operation needed careful piloting and was quite an experience, as there were beautiful houses with extensive lawns on each side. We entered the mouth of the Delaware River and sailed as close inshore as possible until we arrived at our destination, New York, and were directed up the estuary between New Jersey and Staten Island.

I had the chance of an evening ashore, to visit my wife's two uncles who lived in Brooklyn. Their wives told us to take the evening off and have fun, so we took the train into Manhattan. We decided to see a show at Radio City featuring the 'Rockettes', a row of high-kicking girls who gave a stunning performance. We were joined by some American WAVEs who were going on to a bar in Greenwich Village and, as the venue was a favourite haunt of Broadway stars who came in after their shows to sing for the love of it, we had a wonderful time.

Loading in New York did not take long, but it had to be done carefully as there were different kinds of lubricating oil for different purposes. Some was of very superior quality, for high-speed aero engines, and some for motor vehicles; lower grade oil was not mixed with the higher grades.

When loading was completed we anchored in the river waiting to be joined by other ships, some of which were entering from the South. When they had all arrived we set sail under heavy escort, for submarines were still very active at the time.

More than once, soon after leaving port, we ran into dense fog on the banks of Newfoundland where the Greenland cold current met the warmer Gulf Stream. When the fog banks were sighted all ships commenced to stream fog buoys. These were wooden contraptions, each with a metal scoop in the back end. The front was a horizontal vane, angled so as to keep the buoy permanently on the surface, whilst the scoop caused a spout of water to rise about two feet into the air, making it easily visible from a short distance. Even numbers trailed their buoys on one side and odd numbers kept theirs on the other side, so that if possible they could be seen closely alongside the following ship. It was quite an art to try to keep these near to and abreast of the bridge. This all worked well unless someone wandered, thus cutting off a buoy. The ship trailing this might not be aware of it, so extra people would have to be put on lookout.

On one voyage the convoy was three days in dense fog and, even though ships were within a couple of cables of each other, none could be seen. At one point a passenger liner was on our port side and we could hear children laughing and shouting, but the liner was invisible. Eventually we came out of the fog at an angle and saw ship after ship eerily emerging. The fog bank resembled a vertical wall.

Now came the most dangerous period, when the threat from the enemy in the Western Atlantic was at its maximum and it could be a few days before we entered the range of aircraft from home. Usually the first friendly aircraft to be seen would be Sunderland Flying Boats and these were always a very welcome sight.

During one voyage two ships on the starboard wing were torpedoed, but the rest of us arrived safely. As convoys always proceed at the speed of the slowest ship, usually seven knots, it used to take us three weeks to cross. Not a lot of sleep was managed at this time and one always slept fully dressed, with warm clothing handy and a 'crash bag' to hand. My crash bag consisted of 200 cigarettes in a waterproof cloth, as I smoked in those days, 2 boxes of matches in a watertight tin, some photographs and other precious small items. When things happened, speed was of the essence.

At that time my ship, the 'Cymbula', and an Esso Tanker, the 'Comanche' jointly kept Britain supplied with lubricating oils for aircraft, tanks and lorries, etc, bringing in 25,000 tons every six weeks.

On the 9th July 1943 I was promoted to Second Officer and was responsible for navigation. I also became the Gunnery Officer. We made three more trips in convoy to New York without being torpedoed and, on 22nd February 1944 I left the 'Cymbula' for some home leave.

I had been promoted once more, to First Officer, and in March 1944 signed on the MV Dipladon, sailing for the West Indies, to load diesel in Curaçao. We were then ordered to proceed to the Mediterranean to await further orders. As Gibraltar was full of naval ships, we were told to anchor off Oran In North Africa where we waited for a few days before proceeding to Marseille to discharge part of our cargo of diesel and wait again for orders. From information received on the wireless, it was evident that the Allies were liberating the South of France, but encountering stiff resistance.

We proceeded to Toulon, tying up outside a French warship, one of many that had been scuttled so that the Germans could not use them. I was told that some German forces had been cut off and trapped on Toulon Island for several days and a fierce battle had ensued with Senegalese troops, under the command of French officers. It was believed that no Germans had survived to leave the island.

With the assistance of some French operators we managed to connect a pipeline over the warships which in turn connected to another line leading into a tunnel. I went ashore, to find that the area was honeycombed with tunnels and all oil tanks were housed underground. In one tunnel there were four large, high speed diesel engines, the type used in German E-boats: all booby trapped. One had to tread very gingerly, as there were piles of ammunition and guns everywhere and signs warning against mines. Later, as I walked through some small residential streets, I noticed a trickle of French families returning to their homes that had once been beautiful, but were now in a terrible state with graffiti all over the walls.

We left Toulon to proceed along the South Coast of France, oiling various British and American men-of-war, until we received a warning of enemy aircraft. I remember we sighted some planes, but recall nothing that happened afterwards. I must have lost consciousness for a while and was subsequently told that there had been a massive bomb blast.

Once having discharged all our cargo we headed back toward the Caribbean without escort. I became unwell during this passage and it transpired that my previous medical problems had recurred. When we arrived at Galveston, Texas, I was told that I needed surgery. The Company contacted my wife to ask whether she would agree to my entering hospital in America, or whether I should be brought home. Without any hesitation, Gwynneth said "Bring him home".

My journey homeward was by Pullman to New York where I joined the MV Amastra, as acting Master. The Amastra had been fitted out as an MAC ship earlier in the War. The ship had carried three Swordfish planes that had had the particular advantage of being able to take off and land on a short runway. However, after the Battle of the Atlantic had been won, this was discontinued. Our voyage was without incident and we arrived safely in Liverpool.

I soon underwent an operation in Bridgend Hospital and, after three months convalescence, was told to attend the Ministry of Transport doctor. After he had looked at me, then at my history, he stated that he would not recommend me for further sea duties. This was devastating news.

12. Afterword

Being declared unfit for sea duties had been an extremely bitter blow. I doubted whether any part of my experience in my former career would be relevant to securing a new role in life.

While I was still convalescent, the local Collector of Taxes in Bridgend suggested that I might be able to help him. His office was overwhelmed by paperwork generated by claims for War Damages and he felt that a sedentary job might help my recovery. My simple tasks would include handling cheques, issuing receipts and balancing the books. Returning home from the office in the evening I was barely able to settle, let alone eat the meal that Gwynneth had prepared. I would abruptly leave the house again to walk up a local mountainside for some fresh air, so onerous did I find the confinement of office life in those early days.

Learning that some examinations were to take place in Cardiff for entry into the Civil Service, I decided to give them a try. To cut a long story short, I passed, and a long career with the Inland Revenue followed, travelling the length and breadth of the country, making many friends and very few enemies, despite the nature of my work.

My last assignment was to Swindon where we settled happily and I finally retired in 1981. Still active in mind and body, it soon became apparent to my understanding wife that

I was not adapting well to having so much time on my hands, so she encouraged me to welcome an approach from the local VAT Enforcement office. As a result, I worked for three days a week with their officers until I reached the age of seventy-one, enjoying the mix of work and our free time together to the fullest.

Anyone reading this narrative will appreciate that I had a wife that never caused me a day's worry and who was always a joy to me. She died in 1993 and, although I could look after myself, the simplest tasks would cause tears, for I associated everything with her. We had had 54 years, 1 month and 9 days of married life.

Fresh air and the hard manual work involved in maintaining my garden continue to give me great satisfaction; much of the enjoyment being derived from the large surplus of fruit and vegetables that I can give to neighbours and friends. While Gwynneth was unwell I took a Cordon Bleu cookery course that has stood me in great stead and the kitchen is my laboratory for new and exotic dishes. The University of the Third Age provides courses locally, so I am studying French in order to be able to speak it more fluently on my trips there, and my computer has opened up another new sphere of activity. All in all I am glad to say that I have had, and am still having, a very good life.

~ END ~

Index

The Author's mother Ada and wife Gwynneth, Ogmore-by-Sea, 1939.

Crew of the SS *West Wales*, 1936

View from the bridge of MS Glengarry, Indian Ocean, 1936.

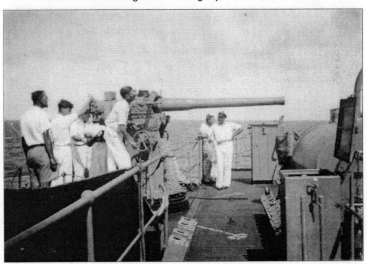

Gunnery practice, MS Glengarry, 1939.

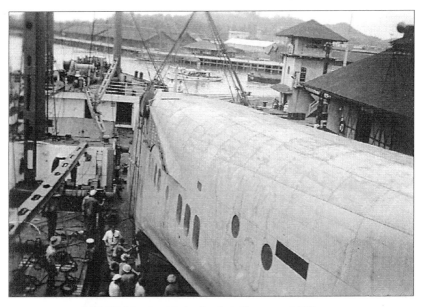

QANTAS flying boat being loaded, Singapore, 1938.

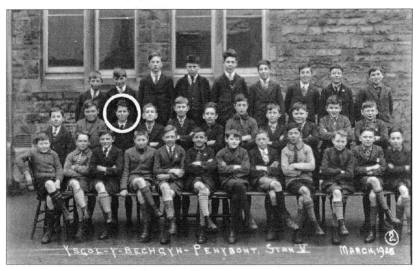

Penybont School, Brigend 1928 (the Author ringed).